LOST
Was the Key

by

Leah A. Haley

Best wishes,
Leah A. Haley

GREENLEAF PUBLICATIONS

Library of Congress Cataloging Data

Haley, Leah A.
　　　Lost was the key / by Leah A. Haley. —— Tuscaloosa, AL: Greenleaf Publications, c1993.

　　　159, [1] p. ; 24 cm.

　　　Includes bibliographical references (p. [160]).
　　　ISBN 1-883729-03-3

　　　1. Unidentified flying objects—sightings and encounters—Alabama. I. Title.

TL789.3.H326　　　1993　　　001.9'42——dc20　　93-215739
　　　　　　　　　　　　　　　　　　　　　　　　　　　　AACR 2 MARC

Library of Congress

Printed in the United States of America

First Edition 1993
Trade Paperback Edition 1995

This book is dedicated to my husband whose patience, understanding, and working extra hours enabled me to concentrate on my writing – and to the numerous other abductees out there.

FOREWORD

As a Licensed Clinical Social Worker, I have provided marriage and family counseling, individual and group therapy, and hypnotherapy for a wide variety of psychiatric disorders over the last fourteen years. I volunteered my time and talents in the field of UFO research to assist those requesting help in determining whether their recalled experiences have any psychiatric basis as a source for their accounts. I have worked with nearly 100 people and have been unable to find a psychiatric disorder which could begin to serve as the origin for all of these amazingly similar tales from such a vastly divergent group of healthy individuals. Symptomatology most frequently reflects the clinical picture of a Post Traumatic Stress Disorder — a disorder which by definition requires an external traumatizing event which is perceived as real by the individual rather than internally generated as in a mental disturbance or emotional conflict. These individuals typically possess good coping skills which are only temporarily de-railed by the extraordinary features and confusing events experienced in UFO encounters. These are the kinds of emotional responses one would expect to see clinically in humans if the experiences are indeed real as they report.

The reported experiences of Leah A. Haley are especially intriguing for many reasons. First, despite having no knowl-edge or clear exposure to UFO abduction reports and data patterns, she produced countless details under hypnosis with strong correlational ties to both published and unpublished data despite leading questions and paradoxical suggestions deliberately designed to produce logical responses which would actually be oppositional to the data found in "abduction scenarios."

Second, I am impressed with her emotional reactions and many attempts to deny the events — sometimes creating peculiar rationalizations as a desperate effort to avoid her own feelings. She kept hoping I could find a psychiatric disorder to explain away her experiences. Ironically, two independent sources of psychological testing confirmed my diagnosis of Post Traumatic Stress Disorder — and *no* insanity.

Third, she was afraid of publicity and demanded confidentiality. She was a woman struggling with frightening new and personal questions. She had always viewed the subject of UFOs with reserved curiosity. She is now convinced of their existence and determined to share these bizarre revelations as a way of educating others, creating an awareness for doubters, and helping those with similar experiences and feelings.

Fourth, her own careful documentation and tireless investigative efforts reflect a determination to find the truth objectively with several clever and bold attempts to verify information retrieved from hypnotic regressions. She was always the first to doubt her own recollections and the last to accept them. She always sought any type of correlating evidence.

Last, her information that strongly suggests governmental intrusion and monitoring does correlate well with other well-documented cases where this has apparently occurred. I called upon the expertise of Leonard Stringfield, Linda Moulton Howe, and Stan Gordon to assist with feedback and guidance in this area of concern. Each of these researchers has a wealth of incriminating data that depicts governmental interest, surveillance, and direct intervention in a great number of UFO cases. None of these sources expressed any significant doubt or sense of disbelief in her accounts. Furthermore, other conscious events with other witnesses present have confirmed without much doubt that people associated with military and governmental agencies are clearly interested in her actions and beliefs.

I conducted all fourteen hypnosis sessions with Leah, assisted by four supportive and knowledgeable UFO investigators: Ann Bayliff, Susan Bedell, Lisa Dusenberry, and Carla Vincel. None of these skilled helpers had any difficulty with the data that spilled forth. I believe Leah to be a sane, concerned, sincere, and intelligent woman who has had the expected emotional and psychological reactions that anyone might have if trying to fit this bizarre phenomenon and its implications into a regular daily routine and "normal" sense of living again. Please open your hearts and your minds to the experiences of Leah A. Haley.

John S. Carpenter, MSW/LCSW

ACKNOWLEDGMENTS

John Carpenter, Ann Bayliff, Susan Bedell, Lisa Dusenberry, and Carla Vincel unselfishly gave many hours of their time for my hypnosis sessions. Thanks also goes to their families for being willing to share them.

Duane Bedell and Seth and Lori Haley trudged through drafts of the manuscript and provided editorial comments and suggestions.

Budd Hopkins responded to my initial cry for help, sent helpful information for me to read, and kindly referred me to a skilled hypnotherapist.

Several kind souls were responsible for the analysis of the strange metal object. I extend to them my sincere thanks.

Don Ware has shared much-needed information, advice, and support. He voluntarily investigated events that may be related to my incident at the beach and, along with Bob Reid, tirelessly accompanied me on a thirteen-mile hike in a search for answers related to this incident.

Linda Moulton Howe and Leonard Stringfield were among the first to hear of my problems with people associated with military and government agencies. Their sincere interest and credence in my story, as well as the examples they set, gave me the strength to continue my investigation into the UFO phenomenon.

Forest Crawford, Stan Gordon, and Leonard Stringfield have unfailingly kept up with every aspect of my case. I owe them special appreciation for their continued concern, support, and interest.

CHAPTER ONE

I will never forget when the world I knew started to crumble. As I contemplate the events that have taken place since then, I can't help but think about Humpty Dumpty and how he couldn't be put back together again. My world and my life are like that. They have crumbled so badly the pieces will never again fit back together the way they were before that weekend.

On Saturday, July 7, 1990, my teenage daughters, Laura and Kelly (pseudonyms), left for church camp.[1] After seeing them off, I drove to my parents' home in North Alabama for a weekend visit. My husband, Mike (pseudonym), who was working out of town at the time, planned to meet me there.

I enjoyed the drive immensely. The national forest and green rolling hills along the latter portion of the drive are beautiful, and I am always thankful when I can escape the bleak flatland of Craston, the small Southern town where I live.[2] By the time I arrived, Mike was already there, his van parked in front of the country grocery store my parents own. Knowing my parents would be working at that time of day, I, too, stopped at the store and went inside. Mike gave me a hug, and Mother and Daddy flashed smiles that let me know they were glad to see me.

That afternoon at my parents' store was not unlike any other I had spent there. Daddy, still spry for his age, rushed out to pump gasoline whenever an automobile pulled up to the pumps. Between gasoline customers he sat inside the store talking to Mike and greeting the old-timers who occasionally wandered in. Because Daddy rarely talks about anything other than fishing and hunting, I sensed he and Mike were cooking up a fishing trip for the next day.

Mother rang up sales at the register. I thought how nice it would be to work as slowly as she did, never getting in a hurry. When Mother didn't have any customers, she and I talked about what we had been doing lately. Mother is an excellent seamstress; she showed me her latest creations and what she planned to make next. I talked with her about all the plans Mike and I had to start construction on a house. I could tell she shared my excitement. Occasionally, I wandered over to where Daddy was sitting and listened to another of his fish stories.

We ate dinner after my parents closed the store for the evening and then watched TV and talked. Daddy and Mike went to bed at a reasonable time, but Mother and I sat up late, trying to cram in as much time together as possible since we seldom saw each other.

Daddy and Mike got up at the crack of dawn Sunday morning and went fishing. Mother and I got up much later. While we ate a leisurely breakfast at the kitchen table, Mother read the local paper. She mentioned that one of the articles stated the Russian government had started to openly admit the existence of UFOs. Then she lamented that she had been unable to finish a book she had borrowed from my sister-in-law Lori (pseudonym) because she and my brother Seth (pseudonym) took it back home with them when they last visited.

I asked, "What kind of book?"

"A book about people from outer space and nonsense like that," she replied.

I wasn't surprised that Mother would think the possibility of extraterrestrial life was nonsense. She was the type of person who sought shelter in the familiar, shying away from any new adventure. But I firmly believed extraterrestrial beings existed and decided to plead my case.

"Mother, I don't understand why you think there can't be intelligent life on other planets. There are so many stars and planets out there and probably thousands we don't even know about. Why would God put people on just one of them?"

"Well, I just don't think He put beings on other planets."

"You *still* don't believe Seth and I saw those spaceships when we were kids, do you?"

"I believe you saw *something*, but not spaceships. They were weather balloons or satellites or something like that. Seth mentioned he might drive over to see you this morning. If he does, we can ask him what he remembers."

"But you or Mr. Goode (pseudonym) called the weather

station and the airport, and nothing was seen on radar. There was no report of weather balloons or satellites or anything else showing up. Don't you remember?"

"Mr. Goode is the one who called. I was too busy doing something else; I don't remember what. I think Lynda (pseudonym) was a baby then. How many things did you see?"

"I think there were three of them. Two or three. I'm pretty sure there were three. It's been such a long time, though, I'm not positive. When I see Seth, I'll ask him if he remembers. All I know is they were blue and silver, and they were round. They stayed in one place in the sky for a long time. Then all but one dashed away instantly, and one landed in the woods. Mr. Goode took us to look for it, but we couldn't find it."

We changed the subject, and I decided to get dressed. While I was putting on my makeup, I heard the kitchen door open and then the sound of Seth's voice, jovial as usual.

Seth has a wonderful sense of humor. He's usually able to cheer me up even when I'm in the worst of moods. I've always been a bit jealous of Seth because while he has never had many material possessions, he always seems to be happy and to find plenty of time to have fun. Despite the jealousy on my part, the two of us get along extremely well. And since I hadn't seen Seth since Christmas, I was glad he was there. But I couldn't wait to get through with the pleasantries so I could ask him about the spaceships.

"Seth, do you remember seeing those spaceships when we were kids living in Gardendale?"

"Oh, yeah! How could I ever forget that?"

"How many do you remember seeing?"

"I only remember seeing one. It stayed in one spot for a long time. Then it sailed to the right and landed behind some trees at the end of the block. You said you had seen two of them shoot off into the sky suddenly, and then the one I saw just soared into the woods and landed. It was silver in color and perfectly round."

"I thought they were blue and silver."

"Well, I think the one I saw was silver but looked blue when the sun hit it a certain way. But you probably remember better than I do because I was only about seven or eight and you were two years older. I do remember the shape, though. It was round."

11

"Do you believe they really were spaceships and that beings from other planets really do come to Earth?" I asked him.

"Yeah. I've read a lot about it. I've also heard the government knows all about this kind of stuff and just won't let the public in on it because it's afraid of mass panic. I've read quite a bit about people having encounters with aliens, too. Some people have had dreams about being abducted by aliens but then under hypnosis supposedly find out the dream wasn't a dream at all."

I thought about the vivid dream I once had about being aboard a spaceship. "Do you believe these people—that they actually did have an encounter with aliens?" I asked.

"Well, from what I've read and seen on talk shows, it seems pretty convincing."

I wondered if I should tell Seth about my dream. That dream had always haunted me because it had seemed so real. If it *was* simply a dream, there would be no harm in mentioning it to Seth. Still, it took me a while to muster up the courage.

"Well," I started slowly. "I want to tell you about a dream I had while we were living in Florence, but you and Mother have got to promise not to laugh. I've never told anybody about this before because I didn't want them to think I'd gone nuts. Do you promise not to laugh or make fun of me?"

"Yeah, I promise," Seth replied.

"Mother?"

She didn't answer, so I repeated my question.

"Okay. I promise not to laugh," she said.

"Well, I dreamed I was in a round room in a spaceship," I told them. "I was lying on a flat platform, like an examining table in a doctor's office. There were little creatures doing things to me."

Seth raised his eyebrows. "What did the creatures look like?" he asked.

"I don't remember them clearly. It's all kind of vague. I'm not very good at judging height, but I'd say they were between four and five feet tall."

"What color were they?"

"I don't remember any distinct color. I think they were sort of neutral. But I remember their eyes. They weren't at all like our eyes. They were real dark with no whites, sort of almond shaped, and they slanted upwards."

"Like an Oriental's eyes?"

"No, not like that. They were much bigger, and they didn't have any pupils. They were really different."

Seth wanted to know what the controls in the spaceship looked like. I told him I didn't remember seeing any controls. He asked what else I remembered.

"That's it. That's all there was to it," I replied.

"Were you afraid?" he asked.

"No. Not during the dream. It was very peaceful. I was just lying there on the platform, and the creatures were doing things to me but I don't remember exactly what. But I *was* afraid the next morning. After I got up, I thought to myself, 'I was in a spaceship last night,' and I was very frightened. But then I asked myself, 'How can a spaceship have been in our subdivision without being seen by the neighbors? And how could the creatures have gotten into the house and taken me out without Mike knowing it?' Besides, I checked, and all the windows and doors were locked. So I *must* have been dreaming."

"You mean the dream seemed so real you had to check the doors and windows in order to convince yourself that it *was* only a dream?"

"Yes."

"Doesn't that seem rather odd to you?"

I thought about it. Yes, it did seem rather odd. I looked over at Mother. As I explained my dream, she turned whiter shades of pale and now she was looking at me oddly.

"Why are you looking at me like that?" I wanted to know.

She didn't answer. I repeated my question and Seth answered for her.

"Because what you described is very similar to what she just read in the book I loaned her. Leah (pseudonym), I think *you* should read some of these books. You need to read the book Mother just read, and you need to read the ones Budd Hopkins wrote."

"You know I don't have time to read books for pleasure," I replied.

I asked Mother if the dream I described was similar to what she had recently read about. She didn't answer.

13

"Is it, Mother?" I asked again. "Tell me the truth."

Finally she spoke. "Yeah, it's similar. But it was just a dream, so forget about it."

"No," I argued. "Now you two have gotten my curiosity up. I want to know if it was just a dream."

"Just drop it, Leah," Mother requested. There was a pleading tone in her voice.

Seth clearly was not about to drop it. He told me some of the people he had read about had physical evidence of their abductions. He asked me if I had any unusual scars or marks on my body.

I told him I have a scar below the back of my knee.

"What does it look like?" Seth asked. "How did it get there? Is it vertical or horizontal?"

"I don't know how it got there. I've always wondered about that, but it looks just like a razor cut. And it's horizontal, I think. I haven't noticed it in a long time. It's probably faded by now."

Seth asked me to pull up my pants leg so he could take a look at the scar. I was unable to pull the leg of my jeans up high enough, so I went into the bedroom and put on some shorts. Then Seth looked for the scar but couldn't find it.

"Well," he said, "if it's horizontal, it probably doesn't mean anything anyway. You really need to read those books. They'll do either one of two things. They'll either scare you so badly that you'll stop reading them or you'll write to Budd Hopkins."

"If you really think this could have been something more than a dream, I don't want to read anything about it yet. I don't want anything confusing me. So don't tell me anything that might interfere with me finding out whether it was really a dream or not."

"Okay." Seth paused for a few seconds and then asked, "Did you have any strange illnesses around the time you had this dream?"

I thought about the time I had to go into the hospital for several days for tests because I was experiencing pain and burning in my kidneys, bladder, and urinary tract. The doctor couldn't find anything wrong, so he told me my problem must be caused by stress. Several months later, I concluded by trial and error that spicy food was causing the problem.

I told Seth all of this and he asked, "Are you sure spicy food was *causing* the problem and not just *aggravating* a problem of some other sort? Do you have trouble with spicy food now?"

"Well, no, but maybe it's because I don't eat a whole lot of it at a time."

"Have you ever had any trouble with nosebleeds or your ears?"

I replied I probably had no more nosebleeds than anybody else. Then I began to describe the pain I frequently experienced in the glands and ear on the right side of my head. The pain occurred only after I had spent several hours either in my home office or in the library. I had finally concluded I must be allergic to something connected to copying machines, maybe the ink.

Seth asked me when these problems originated. I told him they started when we lived in Florence, Alabama, but they didn't get bad until we moved to Craston and I started using duplicating machines so much.

Seth wanted to know if the doctor said I had an allergy.

"No," I told him. "The doctor couldn't find anything at all wrong with me, so he said it must be stress. Doctors are such jerks. Why can't they admit they don't know what the problem is instead of telling people it's just stress? I persuaded him to give me a prescription for allergy medicine even though he didn't think the problem was allergy related. Why are you asking me these questions?"

"Because the aliens do these medical experiments on people, and they put what some people believe may be tracking devices up the nose or in the ear."

"All right, Seth. Stop making fun of me!"

"I'm not making fun of you."

"Yes, you are. You're pulling my leg about all of this stuff."

"Really, Leah, I'm not. Some of the things you've told us are so much like what I've read. The subject of *Intruders* even had a place in her yard where grass wouldn't grow.[3] Did you ever have anything like that in your yard?"

"Yeah, there was a round spot where the grass was brown in our yard in Florence. We never did figure out what caused it."

Mother spoke again. "I remember that. But I think it was in your yard in Tullahoma."

"No. It wasn't there. Maybe it was in Tuscaloosa. Anyway, somewhere I lived there was a round spot where the grass was dead. But what's that got to do with anything?"

"Maybe a spaceship landed there."

"Oh, come on, Seth. This is crazy. This conversation is absolutely ridiculous! I just had a dream. It *had* to have been a dream. It's impossible for it to have been real. Besides, why in the world would creatures want to take *me*?"

"That's what all the other people said."

About this time, Daddy and Mike came back from fishing, so we quickly changed the subject. I whispered to Seth and Mother that they'd better not breathe a word of this conversation to Mike. He would probably think we were all insane.

But I couldn't erase our conversation from my mind. The next morning, after taking a shower, I looked for my scar in the bedroom where there is more light than in the kitchen. I found the scar, but it was barely visible. It was vertical, not horizontal. I showed it to Seth. Then I told my mother. She turned white again. However, Seth said the scar looked like a razor cut. He said the pictures of the scars he had seen in his books appeared to be longer and wider.

Then Seth handed me a piece of paper on which he had been drawing. Goose pimples ran up and down my arms. I closed my eyes and covered my face with a magazine I was holding. It seemed as though I had seen a ghost. What my brother showed me was a picture of a creature like the ones I had seen in the spaceship. After getting over my initial fright, I looked more closely at the picture.

"The head's not right," I said. "Neither are the eyes."

Seth asked me to fix them; I reminded him I can't draw.

"You can try!" he said.

I fixed them to the best of my ability. I told my brother and mother I wanted to write to Budd Hopkins about my experiences to determine whether they were real. My mother again begged me to drop the idea.

After I got home, I decided to take my mother's advice. I told myself again my dream had to have been just a dream. It had to have been. Besides, I didn't have time to deal with this sort of nonsense. I had a full-time job teaching accounting. I was attending graduate school, working on a Master's Degree in Business Administration with plans to pursue my doctorate. And since my husband worked out of town most of the time and lived in motels, I was essentially raising our daughters by myself. I barely had time to sleep, much less take on yet another project.

But no matter what I was doing, I couldn't get the subject out of my mind. I had trouble falling asleep at night. I kept wondering if alien creatures were hiding somewhere watching me. I sat in my graduate school classes drawing the creatures when I should have been listening to the lectures.

After a couple of weeks passed, I finally found enough courage to tell my husband about the conversation that my mother, my brother, and I had when we were at my parents' house. I had dreaded telling Mike because I wasn't sure how he'd react. Mike doesn't talk much, and after almost twenty years of marriage, I still can't figure out what is going on in his mind. Yet, I didn't like keeping secrets from him so when we had a chance to be alone I poured out the details of the conversation I had with Mother and Seth on July 8. My husband listened attentively, unusually attentively for my husband. And he had a strange expression on his face.

"Why are you looking at me like that?" I asked. "You think I'm nuts, don't you?"

Mike explained that was not what he was thinking at all. He told me that last week he had rented the movie *Communion* and watched it in his motel room. He said my dream was very similar to some of the experiences described in the movie. He assured me if I wanted to find out for sure whether my dream was actually a dream or whether it was a real event, he would support me.[4]

With Mike's commitment of support, I called Seth and asked him how I could get in touch with Budd Hopkins. Seth found the address in one of his books and read it to me. Then he told me my adjusted picture of the creature looked more like the ones in Mr. Hopkins' book than the one he had originally drawn. But Seth said again I didn't have the right kind of scar.

On August 20, 1990, I wrote my first letter to Mr. Hopkins, all the while wondering if I had gone completely crazy and if my husband had encouraged me to write the letter just so he would have written evidence that could be used to put me away for life.

17

In the letter I described the conversations I had at my parents' house and later with my husband. Weeks passed by with no response to my letter. Seth told me to be patient, that Mr. Hopkins probably received hundreds of letters every day.

Patience never has been one of my virtues. On October 19, I wrote a second letter asking if my first letter had been received. Finally, toward the end of November, I received an information kit for people who feel they may have had UFO abduction experiences and an Intruders Foundation (IF) bulletin from Budd Hopkins' office.

I read the information kit immediately. It contained extremely interesting and helpful information. There were articles on the pros and cons of exploring possible UFO experiences, on what hypnosis is like, and on support groups and contamination.[5] There was also a note referring me to John Carpenter in Springfield, Missouri.

I felt Springfield, Missouri, was too great a distance to travel to explore dreams about aliens. I was much too busy to make trips like that. At the time, I was even too busy to read the Intruders Foundation bulletin Budd Hopkins had sent to me. During the entire fall semester, I was up to the top of my head in work from my job and my graduate studies. Furthermore, in September we had started construction on our new house, and with my husband out of town most of the time, I was the one who had to oversee the work. Many nights I was getting four hours of sleep or less, so I laid the bulletin aside to read later. Or could it be my busy schedule was the excuse I used to avoid reading the bulletin because subconsciously I was afraid?

The first half of December was hectic as usual and seemed to go as fast as it came. Later in the month, after taking and administering final examinations, I got a chance to relax for a couple of weeks and catch up on neglected tasks. On the night of January 17, 1991, I finally read the IF bulletin I had received in November.

One article mentioned that at the end of an alien abduction experience, a woman woke up and found herself suspended about six inches above her bed.[6] Suddenly I remembered a strange dream I had in October. The main differences between my dream and the story I read about this woman were that I was a couple of feet above my bed rather than six inches, and I was held up by a beam of bright light. All sorts of thoughts came to mind. Did this mean I could have been abducted by aliens? Maybe my dreams hadn't been dreams at all. And if they weren't dreams, that meant the aliens were still coming to get me. They were able to follow me from one state to another when we moved. And they were able to block my memory of the encounters, so I didn't know what they were doing to me.

"Oh, no. Please, God," I prayed. "I don't want it to be true."

The next day I wrote a third letter to Budd Hopkins, begging for his help and asking him to send me a list of investigators, hypnotists, and therapists. I hoped there would be someone on the list who lived closer than Missouri.

The day after I mailed the third letter, January 19, 1991, I realized I couldn't wait any longer. I had to talk to somebody about the alien situation *now*! I remembered the information kit I had received in November contained the phone number of the man in Missouri, as well as his address. I decided to phone him. I was trembling as I pushed the buttons on the phone and my heart was racing wildly. What would I say? Surely the man would think I was crazy.

The voice that answered was female. She said John was out of town and wouldn't be back for several days. My heart fell. What was I going to do? I needed to talk to somebody now. In desperation, I asked if she were John's wife. She answered she was John's wife, Denise. I briefly explained why I was calling and told her I desperately needed somebody to talk with—that I was going crazy if I wasn't there already. I don't remember exactly what she said to me, but she was very kind and caring, and succeeded in calming me down. Then she explained the best way for me to reach her husband once he returned from his trip.

It was the morning of January 23 before I was able to reach John Carpenter. Again, I was trembling and my heart was beating rapidly as I pushed the numbers on the phone. All sorts of thoughts raced through my mind. He would probably think I was crazy. Why shouldn't he? Even *I* had begun to question my sanity. Maybe *he* was crazy. After all, he was involved with alien investigations somehow. What was his occupation? Would he be able to help me? What if he was a kook?

19

John Carpenter answered the phone. I explained who I was and why I was calling. He asked me to briefly describe why I thought I may have had alien encounters. I did so. I made it clear I was upset over the possibility. I don't remember exactly what he said to me, but he didn't sound like a kook. He sounded well educated, experienced in dealing with alien abductees, self-confident, pleasant, and caring. Also, his fees were reasonable. I decided perhaps it would be worth my time and trouble to drive to Springfield to see him.

During the phone conversation that day and another one the next, I learned John Carpenter had seen almost fifty people in connection with alien encounters. Fifty people! Were there really that many people in the United States who had been abducted by aliens? It was hard to believe. I also learned he worked in a hospital with psychiatric patients. That was the impetus I needed to make a firm commitment to drive to Springfield. He was qualified to diagnose me as being insane, he could have me committed to a mental institution, and I could get the help and the rest I so desperately needed. I felt it would be easier for me to find out I was crazy than it would be to find out aliens were abducting me. At least there was a chance something could be done about mental illness.

I told Mr. Carpenter I was willing to undergo hypnosis to explore the possibility of encounters with aliens. I had to find out whether my alien-related dreams were really dreams or actual events. Whatever the outcome, I had to know the truth.

A couple of days after our second phone conversation, I received a letter from him along with an explanation of hypnosis. In the letter Mr. Carpenter stated many people like myself had called or written him feeling perplexed and uneasy. He assured me many others had gone through these same sorts of feelings and had learned more about themselves as a result. He asked me to pick several possible weekends I could travel to Springfield.

Mr. Carpenter also included some questionnaires for me to complete. He asked me to include sketches, diagrams, etc., along with a narrative of any sightings or dreams I had experienced. He stressed the more detail I could provide consciously, ahead of our meeting, the more we would be likely to accomplish during my trip.

The letter was comforting and reassuring. It took several days for me to compile the information requested. Once I had it ready, I sent it with a letter describing what had been churning around in my mind.

The more I thought about the prospect of aliens visiting me, the more confused I got. One minute I thought the prospect of aliens actually coming anywhere near me was absurd. The next minute I questioned why my dreams were similar to those of other people. The next minute I again thought I must be going crazy to even consider my dreams were anything other than dreams. My thoughts and feelings were becoming increasingly disturbing. I could no longer sleep well, and, therefore, I remained tired all of the time.

To make matters worse, I had recently experienced two alien-related dreams. The first one occurred December 22, 1990. I dreamed I was outside watching spaceships float down to Earth from the sky. I looked up at them and, knowing they were coming after me, I cried out, "Leave me alone. Please, please, *please*, just go away and leave me alone."

The second dream occurred around the last of January or first of February, 1991. I was hovering above my bed again, but this time there was no beam of bright light holding me up. I extended my arm downward to make sure the bed was a couple of feet below me. It was. Then I thought, "You aliens are *not* going to zap my brain this time. I am going to remain alert. I am going to remember every detail about how you get me out the window or however it is that you get me out of this house." But I woke up without remembering the details I had vowed not to forget.

I described these dreams in my letter to Mr. Carpenter. I also told him my family planned to move into our new house on February 7 and because it would take me a while to get things in order after that, the best time for me to visit him would be during my spring break in March. Furthermore, if I could make the trip then, my brother might be able to accompany me.

Mr. Carpenter phoned me to say the dates of my spring break would work well for him. I phoned Seth and made sure he could accompany me. He didn't have the money to go, but I bribed him by promising to pay all of his expenses. He said if nothing came up he would be glad to go with me. I prayed nothing would come up. I needed the moral support. My husband definitely would not be able to go with me. He is self-employed, and if he doesn't work, he doesn't get paid. We needed the money he could earn to finance my trip.

In February I received a message from Budd Hopkins' office with the name and address of an investigator who lives on the Gulf Coast of Mississippi. Although the drive would take only six hours versus the ten hours it would take to drive to Missouri, I decided to continue with my plans to meet with Mr. Carpenter. After talking with him several times on the phone, I sensed we would get along well, and he seemed to be sincerely interested in helping me. I decided to stick with my plans to drive to Springfield with my brother. We were to leave on March 8.

The weeks passed quickly. I taught four different upper-level accounting courses each semester. Preparing for all of those classes left me very little free time. After we moved into our new house in early February, I spent most of what free time I had cleaning, unpacking boxes, and getting settled. I spent my remaining free time in high school gymnasiums watching Kelly's basketball games. I didn't have much opportunity to think about aliens and spaceships. Yet the subject was almost always in the back of my mind.

I didn't talk about the subject with anyone in my hometown other than my best friend Judith (pseudonym) who swore not to tell anyone except her husband. Everyone would think I was crazy. I might lose my job. My daughters' reputations would be ruined. When my students and colleagues asked about my spring break plans, I replied I was going to Springfield, Missouri, to do some research for a possible book about personal experiences. What was I supposed to say, "I'm going to Springfield, Missouri, to find out whether I've been abducted by creatures from outer space"? I would be laughed out of town. I tried to give a truthful reply. At the time, I didn't know whether I had actually had encounters with aliens, but I thought if I found out such encounters had occurred, then I *might* want to write about them someday. At any rate, that's how I tried to justify the reply I gave when someone asked how I planned to spend spring break.

CHAPTER TWO

Prior to my trip to Springfield, Missouri, few people knew about the possibility that I had experienced encounters with aliens. Of course, Mother, Seth, and Mike knew. Seth told his wife. Mother told Daddy and my sister. Mike told no one. And I told my friend Judith.

In August, 1990, soon after the illuminating conversation that Seth, Mother, and I had at my parents' kitchen table, I met my friend Judith for lunch. Judith and I had met in a graduate class soon after I moved to Craston in August, 1988. Judith's husband, an Air Force officer, had just recently been transferred to Craston.

It was only natural Judith and I would hit it off. Most of the students in our classes were in their early twenties, and Judith and I, being much older, stuck out like sore thumbs. Both of us were new to the area, had been born in the South, and had lived in many places. More importantly, both of us were trying to raise families and go to school at the same time, struggling to improve our financial and career situations. We could commiserate with each other.

During the long lunch I had with Judith that day, I recounted the conversation with my mother and brother concerning spaceships and aliens. Judith listened patiently and with interest. One of the things I liked about Judith was that she really listened when I told her something; she didn't just pretend to be interested like many people do. I knew no matter what I wanted to discuss with Judith I could always count on her genuine interest and concern. And I could count on her to keep my secrets. I felt I could tell Judith anything and she would understand.

After completing my story, I asked Judith what she thought about the situation. She told me she knew I wasn't crazy and she felt the universe was too big not to have beings exist on a planet other than our own. She also told me her husband was extremely interested in the subject of extraterrestrial life, and she asked permission to tell him my story. I gave my permission on the condition that she make her husband promise not to tell anyone else.

From the time we first became acquainted, Judith and I made a point of meeting each other frequently for lunch. Splurging on long lunches was the reward we gave ourselves for studying so hard and maintaining A's in our coursework. I always enjoyed the conversations we shared. So many Craston residents are still living in the past, mourning the loss of the Civil War and the demise of slavery, and wallowing in racial prejudice. But Judith isn't like that. Judith, an extremely intelligent woman, strongly supports equality and progress. It was refreshing to listen to her ideas. Since we met often and I trusted her, I continued to pour out all of my thoughts about the possibility of extraterrestrial visitations. I confided the prospect of having been abducted and not re-membering it frightened and intrigued me at the same time. After all, if creatures actually had abducted me, they appar-ently had done me no harm, and had always returned me. But it was hard for me to understand how things like that could happen without a person remembering it. Judith's opinion was that beings advanced enough to visit Earth probably would be capable of doing many things beyond our realm of understanding. She had a point.

Not only did I keep Judith up to date on my interest in the alien question, I also talked with her about most other as-pects of my life as well. In September, 1990, two months after Seth and I discussed our childhood UFO sighting, a variety of strange incidents began to occur, incidents which made me increasingly uneasy, and I confided in Judith about these things. I began to feel as if I were being followed. Occasionally, a white car seemed to be following me home; at other times it was a dark blue car. I couldn't prove the cars were following me. I just had a gut feeling they were. And I felt as if I were being watched most of the time. I felt uneasy even in my own home. I asked Judith if she had ever felt as if she were being followed. She said yes, that she felt as if she were followed for an entire week once, and she discovered later she actually *had* been followed by FBI agents. Her husband was being investigated for a special security clear-ance at the time.

One unsettling incident occurred in a restaurant. One weekday evening in September my husband phoned to tell me he was coming home for the night. As there was very little food in the house, I suggested we go out for dinner. Mike agreed to meet our daughters and me at a restaurant in town. We lingered over dinner since it is rare for all four of us to eat a meal together. Across from our booth sat two men with short hair. They were dressed in casual but neat attire. Both of them had lean but strong-looking bodies, indicating the men obviously made a point of staying in top physical condition. I probably wouldn't have noticed them, but every time I looked up from my plate, I discovered they were staring at my family. Whenever I looked up, they looked down. Kelly also noticed their behavior. She kicked Laura under the table and said those men were giving her the creeps. Although our dinner was lengthy, the two men were still in the restaurant when we left.

Not long after the restaurant incident, another event upset me. I was working in my office at Craston University. Except for myself, the end of the building in which I worked was deserted. I frequently worked in my office when everyone else was gone because I could get much more work done when no students or colleagues were around to interrupt me. I was trying to get caught up when I glanced up from my paperwork and noticed a handsome young man standing in the doorway. He had short hair and an excellent build and was dressed nicely. He seemed to be studying me, looking me over from head to toe. Then he looked around my office. I asked if I could help him. Feeling extremely uneasy, I unobtrusively worked open my desk drawer and grasped a pair of scissors as I awaited his answer. Considering the type of look he was giving me, the only conclusion I could reach about his presence was that he was there to rape someone and I was a convenient target. I thought to myself, "If you take one step toward me, these scissors are going straight through your chest." I had already picked out my spot. Finally he asked me a few questions. I was so unnerved by his presence that later I couldn't remember what he had asked other than who I was and what my job responsibility was. He asked me some other question that made no sense in the context of that university's operations. After I told him I was unable to answer that question, he left. A sigh of relief rushed from my mouth as I released my grip on the scissors and shut the drawer.

Probably these incidents in and of themselves wouldn't have concerned me so much, but other odd things also began to happen. I came home one day during the fall and discovered the deadbolt lock on the carport door was loose. It looked as if perhaps someone either had tried to pry it open or had removed and replaced it. After entering the house, I got an odd feeling someone had been in there, but I found nothing out of place and nothing missing. If someone wanted to get in the house, why not simply break a window? Perhaps the lock had been loose for some time and I just hadn't noticed it. I tried to console myself with that thought. But the consolation didn't last long. I started hearing odd noises on the telephone. Sometimes clicking sounds, sometimes other phones ringing in the background, sometimes music. And at other times I heard a faint sound like a cassette tape winding slowly around a reel.

In December, I suddenly became frightened to drive alone after dark. I welled up with fear each time I saw the glare of lights in my rear-view mirror. I couldn't understand the source of my fear, which increased when I drove down the roads near my home. I was glad we would soon be moving and I would no longer have to travel down those roads.

We moved into our new home on February 8, 1991. At first our phone lines sounded clear. Then after approximately a week, the old familiar noises returned.

Adding to my frustration, our security system failed to work properly for weeks after we moved into our new house. Repairmen came almost daily. They would fix the alarm; it would soon malfunction again. They were unable to determine the exact cause of the problem and became almost as frustrated over the situation as I was.

On March 5, I came home from the university much earlier than usual. I brought a load of textbooks home so I could work without interruption. It was approximately 11:00 a.m. After entering the house from the garage and turning off the alarm system, I heard a noise that sounded as if it came from the game room, above the garage. Furthermore, I had a gut feeling someone was up there. But I tried to brush away my uneasiness by telling myself I was simply getting paranoid because of all the other odd events taking place. I continued through the sun room and reached the kitchen door which was secured with a deadbolt lock. The lock was loose. I hadn't noticed it being loose when I locked it that morning before going to work. Now I was really frightened. I tried to figure out what to do. Should I call the sheriff? If the person in the game room was a murderer, robber, or rapist, why didn't he emerge and attack me rather than hide? And how had he managed to get in without setting off the alarm? Since I wasn't attacked immediately and because of the other odd events that had occurred recently, I concluded the person must be some sort of government agent who hadn't expected me to arrive home so soon. If this were the case and I called the sheriff, I might find myself in serious trouble. The agent could simply flash his badge to the sheriff and offer a plausible explanation for being in my house, an explanation that would make *me* out to be the criminal. I decided not to make the call. Besides, I wasn't positive anyone actually was hiding in the game room. If the sheriff came out to investigate and found no one up there, I'd feel like an idiot.

I didn't know what to do. I tried once again to tell myself I was imagining things and jumping to conclusions. But still feeling rather uneasy, I decided not to go up to the second floor of the house just yet. If there was an intruder inside, I would have a better chance of escaping if I stayed on the lower level where there were four exterior doors. I made several trips to the garage to get the textbooks I had brought home. Then I did a few household chores. But I constantly looked over my shoulder as I performed these tasks. Around 1:00 p.m. I made myself some lunch and sat down in the den to watch TV while I ate. I usually turn off the TV after watching *As the World Turns*. That particular day I couldn't bear the silence, so I left it on for a little while longer. Shortly after 2:00 p.m., as I left the den and entered the hallway, I heard a beep that startled me. It sounded like the beep our security system makes when someone opens a door or a window. But could the sound have come from the TV? I wasn't sure. However, I knew if the sound resulted from someone leaving the house, at least he had left without harming me. I had been home for three hours and had not been hurt, so I now felt safe enough to go upstairs and do some work. As soon as I took an armful of books upstairs, I heard another unidentifiable sound. Thinking it sounded like a dump truck just outside, I looked out the front upstairs windows to see where the truck was. I saw no truck nor any other object from which that sound could have originated. I ran to the windows at the back of the house and looked out. Still, I saw nothing unusual. Where could that sound have come from? It wasn't until many weeks later when Mike opened the back garage door that I realized the sound must have been the result of someone opening and closing it. The sound of the door going up and down resembles the sound of a dump truck.

I kept telling myself all of these strange incidents were purely coincidental. I was merely being more sensitive than usual because I was unnerved over the possibility aliens had abducted me at some point in my life. I was just being paranoid. But deep down I knew the truth I didn't want to accept. I knew I had been followed. I knew someone had tampered with my locks. And I knew someone had been in my house on March 5.

But why? Why? These strange incidents didn't begin until September—after the conversation with Mother and Seth—after I wrote the first letter to Budd Hopkins describing my possible experiences with aliens—and after I discussed the subject of alien abductions with Judith and Mike. Were these odd incidents related to my inquiries about extraterrestrial life? If so, who else knew about my interest in the subject, how did they find out, and why were they interested in me? I hoped my upcoming trip to Springfield would answer these questions.

CHAPTER THREE

On the morning of March 8, 1991, I eagerly prepared for the trip to Springfield. I left Kelly and Laura a list of instructions and asked a friend and my mother to check on them while I was out of town. After teaching my accounting classes, I stopped at the grocery to pick up a few additional items Kelly and Laura would need while I was gone. I arrived home from work late.

I was still packing when Seth arrived. Neither of us had eaten lunch, so I asked Seth to look in the refrigerator and find us something to eat while I finished getting my clothes together. By the time we finished eating and loading up the car, it was 2:00 p.m. Finally we were on our way.

I was glad Seth was accompanying me. He is talkative, jovial, and fun to be around. Despite the seriousness of our trip, I knew we would enjoy ourselves at least part of the time.

As we drove, we talked about a variety of things, told jokes, and sang along with Seth's Nitty Gritty Dirt Band tapes. At one point, Seth started singing "We're off to see the Wizard, the wonderful Wizard of Oz" because we expected illuminating answers from John Carpenter, whom we subsequently nicknamed "Oz."

After travelling for more than six hours, Seth and I found a motel where we could spend the night. To save money, we rented only one room. The clerk, apparently thinking we were husband and wife, asked if we preferred a king-size bed or two double beds. She chuckled when we told her we didn't practice incest.

We drove into Springfield the next day. As soon as we arrived, we phoned John Carpenter and set up a meeting for early that afternoon. Mr. Carpenter offered to pick us up at the hotel, but I told him if he would give us directions, Seth and I could find the office where he planned to meet us.

We found the building easily and arrived a bit early. No one was in the office where we were to meet, so we found some chairs in an adjoining hallway, sat down, and waited. To pass the time, Seth and I discussed what I expected John Carpenter to look like based on my previous phone conversations with him. I expected him to have blonde or reddish-blonde hair and to be about 5'9" with an average build.

After a few minutes, a man entered the rear door of the building. He was carrying a lounge chair and a sleeping bag.

"That's him," Seth said.

I told Seth I didn't think so. That man had dark brown hair and was taller than the man I had imagined. And surely he wasn't carrying that lounge chair and sleeping bag for me to be hypnotized on. A person undergoing hypnosis is supposed to have a leather couch!

"I bet it is," Seth declared.

"That can't be him," I replied. But the man did go down the hall toward the office where Mr. Carpenter had told us to meet him.

After a few minutes, Seth and I got up from our seats and went down the hall to see. Yes, the man had gone into the appointed office.

"Oh, great," I thought, "Here I've come over four hundred miles to be hypnotized by a man who doesn't even have a couch."

We asked the man if he was John Carpenter. He replied that he was, and Seth and I introduced ourselves. There was no turning back now.

I don't remember what we talked about at first, but I do remember I was extremely nervous. After a few minutes, one of John Carpenter's assisting investigators joined us and we again introduced ourselves.[7] Mr. Carpenter rearranged some furniture and set up the lounge chair, laying the sleeping bag on top of it. We continued to talk while he did this. I kept waiting for him to say it was okay to call him John, but he never did. I was taught at an early age not to call an authority figure by his first name until he grants his permission. I decided to disregard that rule in this situation. I was about to bare my soul to this person. Surely it would be okay to call him by his first name.

John indicated I was to sit in the lounge chair. Having seen no couch, I had already reached that conclusion. Nervous, I sat down and mumbled that I wished I had a security blanket. Grace, John's investigative assistant, said she had a quilt in her automobile and graciously offered to let me use it. I accepted her offer.

After everyone else sat down, John hooked up a microphone and turned on his tape recorder. He told me to relax and explained he was ready to start taping our discussion.

John began the session by asking if I had any trouble sleeping. I explained I usually woke up around 4:00 a.m. and then had trouble falling back asleep. Then John asked Seth and me to tell him about the day we saw spaceships in Gardendale, Alabama.

Seth told John he remembered standing on the front porch of our house and seeing only one object. He knew another neighborhood child was present, but he couldn't remember which one, probably Philip Goode (pseudonym). Then Seth described the setting as he indicated locations on a hand-drawn map of the neighborhood.

"The object was about a city block away," Seth explained. "There was a wooded area and creek south of our house and a wooded area to the east. There were pastures and a wooded area to the north. We watched the object move to the right and go down around the wooded area. Mr. Goode drove us down there. I remember driving down there, I remember sitting in the back seat of the car, and then I remember being back home. And that's all I can remember about it. I know we went looking for it, but we couldn't find it."[8]

John asked Seth if he remembered what time of day we saw the object.

"Seems to me it was in the middle of the day," Seth replied. "The sun was up. It was bright."

I interrupted. "Or afternoon before Daddy came home. He came home early, about 3:00 or 4:00."

John asked what Mr. Goode said about the object or thought it was. Seth explained he didn't remember Mr. Goode's reactions; he remembered only that Mr. Goode drove us to the woods and helped us look for it.

John asked about the size of the object. Seth replied it was probably less than twenty feet in diameter and that it reminded him of a silver Christmas tree ornament hanging in the sky. Then Seth pointed out I had seen more than one.

I told John I thought there were three. All but one darted

upward and away, vanishing instantly. The one remaining floated down into the woods. Mr. Goode took us to look for it, we didn't find anything, and we went back home.

John asked me to describe the next strange incident I could remember. I mentioned the dream I had discussed with Seth and Mother back in July. I explained the event took place in Florence, Alabama, where we lived from 1975 to 1981. I had included a description of this dream in a letter to John, but he asked me to briefly go over it again.

I felt silly sitting there among strangers discussing a dream about a spaceship, but I reluctantly went on.

"Walking down the hall one morning, the thought came to me, 'I was in a spaceship last night.' I don't even know how I knew it was a spaceship. I just remember I was in a round room, lying flat on my back on a platform, like an examining table at a doctor's office. My feet were toward the center of the room. Little creatures were standing around me. They did things to me, but I don't remember what. There was another creature on the other side of the room who kept turning and looking at me and then turning and looking at the other creatures. No word was ever spoken. It seemed as if they knew what each other was thinking, as if there was some kind of understanding between them. I remember thinking how gracefully and effortlessly the creature on the other side of the room moved. The creatures didn't have any ears. I don't recall seeing a mouth. I saw big, dark eyes and two little holes for a nose. I don't remember anything vividly other than big, dark eyes. There's nothing else to it. But the morning I recalled the event, I said to myself, 'No. I couldn't have been in a spaceship. That's ridiculous, to even conceive an idea like that. It seems so real, but it couldn't have been. I live in a subdivision. There are houses all around.' Then I checked all the windows and doors and made sure they were locked. Finally I said to myself, 'See. It couldn't have been real. It had to be a dream. There's nothing else it could have been.' So I told myself to forget it."

Seth interjected, "Don't forget what you told me about losing track of time."

"Oh, you mean with Jeff Krueger (pseudonym)? That was nothing."

"Well, let's hear about it," John requested.

"Okay," I said reluctantly. "This occurred in Huntsville, Alabama. I had a steady boyfriend. We'd go out on a date, we'd go to a movie, and then we'd go parking at the end of a road where there were no houses. And one night the time just disappeared. All of a sudden Jeff looked at his watch and said, 'Oh, my God, I'm going to get killed! It's time to go home.' And we both looked at each other with quizzical expressions on our faces because we couldn't understand what happened to the time. Maybe we fell asleep for a little while. Or maybe we were having so much fun we didn't realize how much time was passing."

"That's possible," John agreed. "How much time would you say did pass?"

"Well, it was about an hour that seemed to be lost. Maybe an hour and a half."

Next John asked me to describe in greater detail the two recent dreams involving my bed I had written him about.

I told him that in the first dream I was lying face down approximately two feet above my bed and a beam of light was holding me up. I was thinking I had to get back into bed so I could get up and get ready for work, but I couldn't move. My brain was working, but my body wasn't. The next thing I knew, my head hit the pillow and I woke up.

In the second dream, scenes jumped from one place to another. In one scene, I was outside, looking up at the stars and thinking, "I've got to go back inside." But the next thing I knew, I was in a conference room talking to people about UFOs. In the third scene, I was above the bed again, but I didn't remember a beam of light this time. As I lay above the bed, I was thinking, "I am not going to let you creatures zap my brain. You are *not* going to zap my brain. I am going to remember every detail of how you get me out that window or however the heck you get me out of this house. I'm going to remember it." But I didn't.

I indicated I felt as if the first dream was an actual event, but the second one had to be merely a dream because I don't make a habit of going to conference rooms in the middle of the night.

John and Grace asked me to describe the conference room in more detail. When I finished, John's comment was, "Well, I don't see too much difference between the dreams that seem real and those that don't."

33

John asked if I had any physical problems after any of these dreams.

I told him about the time I went into the hospital for tests, and since the doctor was unable to determine the cause of the problem, he told me it must be stress. I explained to John I was continually under stress; if stress had caused my problem, I should be sick every day.

I also told John about having a problem with my right ear. He asked me to describe it in more detail.

I told him that occasionally I get a pain that starts in my neck and goes behind and inside my right ear and sometimes into the eye area. The first time I had any trouble with my ear was in the seventies when we lived in Florence, Alabama, but the problem didn't get bad until we moved to Craston. I explained that since the problem occurred only when I had been duplicating papers in my home office or in the college library, I concluded I was allergic to copying ink.

John and Grace seemed amused at my explanation. John asked if I could think of any other dream or incident of any kind that seemed unusual or troublesome. At that point, Seth urged me to tell John and Grace about the dream I had discussed with him on the drive up. I didn't want to tell them. The dream was too embarrassing. Nevertheless, Seth persuaded me to discuss it with them.

Reluctantly, I admitted there was one last dream that seemed real. I recalled having sex with what I called "a spirit of some kind" shortly after I had a hysterectomy in 1981. I didn't remember what the spirit looked like or what the experience felt like. I merely remembered thinking it couldn't have been a spirit of God because I wasn't good enough, so it must have been an evil spirit. And I remembered being thankful I couldn't get pregnant.

Satisfied that we had covered all my pertinent conscious recollections, John indicated we were ready for hypnosis. He asked me if I needed to go to the rest room before we got started. I said it might be a good idea, so we took a short break.

While I was gone to the rest room, I thought how nice it was to have someone considerate of my needs for a change. At home I was always the one who had to take care of everyone else's needs. I decided I liked John and Grace. They

were professional, friendly, and easy to talk to. Maybe it wasn't so important to have a couch to lie on after all.

After everyone got back into the room, we discussed a few more things before beginning hypnosis. I mentioned I had recently become extremely distressed each time I drove alone at night and saw street lights reflecting in my rear-view mirror. There was no rational reason for me to experience such fear. Then I related the other matters that had made me feel uneasy: the cars following me, the men who watched my family in the restaurant, the young man I thought was going to rape me in my office, the loosened door locks, the problems with our new security system, and the noise in the game room when I came home from work early last Tuesday.

Feeling we had covered every topic of importance, John announced, "Okay. Well, now we do the fun part. This is where you get to relax. After we get through the relaxation part and start looking at some of these images and different things that you remember, it'll be very easy for you to think, 'Oh, I'm not going to say that. That'll sound stupid.' Or, 'No, I'm just imagining that. I'm not going to say it.' What I want you to have is, you know, the term 'stream of consciousness' where you say whatever comes to your mind. Instead of editing it, just lay it out and let us edit it. Okay? In other words, just say whatever does cross your mind or does hit you, anything peculiar or odd. Even if it's just a flash of something that you think is just totally bananas, just go ahead and say it anyway."

What I wanted to say at that moment was, "Let me out of here. I've decided to forget the whole thing. I don't want to be hypnotized. I don't want somebody poking inside my mind. This whole idea was a big mistake."

But there is one side of me that will try almost anything once. Besides, Seth and I had driven too great a distance for me to give up now. And if I went through this one hypnosis session, perhaps we would find out all of my dream-like images were merely dreams, and my confusion and worries would be over.

Being so nervous, I found it difficult to relax. But John was very good at making me feel comfortable. At first he had me focus on a point in the ceiling. When my eyes got tired and heavy, he told me I could close them. That felt good.

John's voice was steady, calm, soothing. He instructed me to find my voice and to think about the house I lived in as a child in Gardendale, Alabama. Then he began to ask me questions about it.

I began describing my childhood home. I was both pleased and surprised to remember the minute details I had forgotten over the years: the white ornamental metal on the front screen door; the mimosa tree that I pulled the little beans from; the front sidewalk where I played school with my marbles and Chinese checker board; four-o'clocks and a pomegranate tree in the back yard; inside the house, the floor furnace that was in the middle of the hallway; the shiny hardwood floors; and my walking doll, Betsy, lying on my bed. Interesting, until that moment I had forgotten her name.

Next John asked me to remember the day when Seth, some other neighborhood kid, and I saw something up in the sky that caught my eye.

"Think about how you came to notice it," John said. "Whether you saw it first or as you stand there on the porch who might be talking or saying something about it."

I remembered after much concentration that I was the one who saw the objects first, three of them sitting stationary in the bright blue sky. They were round and silver and were in a triangular formation, with one of the objects appearing a bit more distant than the others. Sometimes the sun would glare on the objects in such a way that parts of them looked bluish. I watched them for a long time. Suddenly two of them darted upward to the north, vanishing instantly from sight. Philip Goode and Seth joined me, and we watched the third object hover for a long time before floating over the trees to our right and disappearing into the woods.

After the object landed in the woods, Philip, Seth, and I ran up the street to Philip's house and told his father that a flying saucer landed in the woods and we wanted to go find it. He could tell we were serious because fear was mixed in with the excitement in our voices. We all climbed into Mr. Goode's old car, drove down the street, and parked in the grass near the woods. When we got into the woods, we scattered out. I set out to our right.

What I remembered next both surprised and frightened me. Next to a big tree I saw a creature with a weird-looking face and big, black eyes. The eyes looked so different from ours, without eyeballs and without eyelashes. The body was a chalky color. The top part of the head was much wider than the bottom. The creature had no hair. He was about the same height as I was. He stood still and kept staring at me with those huge eyes. As I looked deep into those eyes, I could tell the creature didn't want me to be afraid.

My next memory was of being in a different part of the woods and seeing a beam of bright light, like a bunch of sunrays all together, coming towards me. I also saw a round, silver object hovering above the ground in a clearing.

"Did you want to run now?" John asked.

"I wanted to go in it," I replied.

I didn't remember how I got into the hovering object, but I soon remembered being in it and lying on a platform inside a circular room. Several other creatures were there. I was surprised that they all looked alike. Their eyes told me not to be afraid. And I wasn't; I felt completely at peace. The room was brightly lit, although I couldn't remember seeing the source of the lighting.

"What are you wearing at this point?" John asked.

I was shocked to discover I had on nothing at all. Then I remembered looking at the creatures' hands, discovering their fingers were longer than ours and they had only four. One of the creatures used a needle-like instrument to poke my arms, legs, and feet. I noticed the instrument was silver and approximately a foot long.

"Well, I think I would have jumped and run at that point!" John exclaimed as I described this procedure.

"No, I'm not afraid," I stated calmly.

The next thing I remembered was that I had rejoined my friends and we were all leaving the woods, disappointed we hadn't found the flying saucer.

John asked me if I ever remembered seeing the creature again. Although I tried very hard, I couldn't remember anything else, so John slowly and gently brought me out of the hypnotic state.

As I emerged from my unusually relaxed state, I was more confused than ever. Did these things actually happen? Was my mind playing tricks on me? Had I truly gone crazy? Perhaps I had already been committed to a mental ward somewhere and everything that passed through my mind was an illusion. I didn't know. If the encounter with the creature actually had taken place, why hadn't I remembered all of it consciously before now?

I began to verbalize my thoughts. I denied being hypnotized and stated the story I told resulted from my husband planting it in my brain.

"Right," John said with an amused tone. "He did a good job then. What did he tell you?"

"He said, 'Maybe you saw a spaceship when you were little and didn't remember.'"

"Well, that sure implanted it in your brain, didn't it?" John said.

"Well, it did. I mean, I conjured it all up," I replied, not wanting to accept the reality of the encounter.

"Right," John said in a way that let me know he did not accept my explanation. "We'll tell you all your details are right on the money. Grace and I are sitting here predicting what you're going to say before you say it."

"But I didn't remember everything," I argued.

"You don't have to remember everything," John said. "Besides, that can still happen."

I could only manage to say, "I could use a strawberry daiquiri now."

John asked me to draw a picture of the creature I had met face-to-face in the woods. I tried to the best of my ability to draw it, but I couldn't get it just right. I promised to try to do a better job later at the hotel. We all agreed to meet first thing in the morning for another hypnosis session. We said goodbye and left.

After leaving the building, Seth and I drove to a restaurant John had recommended. There was a long line. Too hungry and tired to wait, we tried a different restaurant. The same situation existed there, so we decided to go back to the hotel and order room service. We finally ended up, however, in the hotel dining room. Our order arrived probably in the same amount of time we would have been served if we had remained at the first restaurant and waited our turn. Just my luck.

I didn't feel like eating anyway. My head was spinning. Today I found out that as a child I had been abducted by aliens and all this time it had been blocked from my memory. It didn't make sense. How could that happen? I didn't understand. Surely I was crazy. How did I know I wasn't at this very moment in a mental institution somewhere imagining this whole trip? The answer was that I didn't know it. Thoughts kept going around and around in my mind. Questions led to more and more questions. I was glad Seth was there. I tried to convince Seth I wasn't hypnotized because I knew what was going on around me the whole time my eyes were closed. Seth, in turn, tried to convince me I was hypnotized. He said he could tell by the way my eyes moved and by my facial expressions and emotions.

After dinner, Seth and I retired for the night. I knew I wouldn't be able to sleep very well with so much on my mind but I had to try.

CHAPTER FOUR

The next morning arrived quickly, and I was exhausted. I had tossed and turned all night, trying to digest the events of the previous day. After breakfast, Seth and I met John and Grace for my second hypnosis session. John turned on the tape recorder. We began discussing what I had been thinking about since last night's session.

First I told John and Grace that late last night I remembered the alien I saw as a child in Gardendale took me by the hand shortly after we established eye contact. He led me through the woods, displaying a sense of comradeship.

Then I explained that when I went in for my annual gynecological checkup in the fall of 1989, I had numerous bruises on my arms and legs and had no idea how they had gotten there. My gynecologist sent me to a lab to have various tests performed, but the results shed no light on why I might be bruising like that.

Next we talked about the red spot on the white of my left eye. It appeared overnight when I was a child living in Gardendale, Alabama. Mother took me to the doctor who said the redness was probably due to a broken capillary and it should be gone in a few days. But it never did disappear, and its presence has always disturbed me.

Then I explained how I sometimes heard the sound of something breathing underneath our house in Florence, Alabama. The sounds resembled human breathing.

"What time of day or night did you usually hear it?" John asked.

"I don't remember," I answered. "Laura and Kelly were active toddlers then. I occasionally would go into the living room to rest. I heard the breathing under the floor where I sat. The foundation of the house was about four feet high on that end."

"How long did that go on?" Grace asked.

"For weeks. Then we moved to Tuscaloosa. I kept telling my husband to come in and listen to it, and he'd come in and say, 'I don't hear anything.'"

Grace asked if my husband or I had looked under the house to see whether anything was there.

"*He* did," I replied. "But he didn't see anything."

"Hmm," John said. "I kind of doubt you'd find anything. Some old guy living down there, you know."

"Mike kept telling me it was chipmunks."

"You don't hear chipmunks breathing," John said. "I don't think you could if you tried."

After this preliminary discussion it was time for hypnosis to begin. I was extremely nervous about going through hypnosis again, but John was able to help me relax. He directed me to remember a time when I was near my bed, but not exactly in it. He then asked me to describe my first recollections about this experience.

I began by describing the cross-stitched picture that hangs over my bed. It says, "Sweet Dreams" and is bordered with morning glories. I've always loved that picture. But I didn't like remembering being in that bedroom on the day John asked me to remember, so I jumped to the bedroom of our previous home in Florence, Alabama, and started describing it.

I explained I didn't have the cross-stitched picture when we lived in that house. Instead, we had short windows above the bed. I hated those windows because to open them we had to push them out rather than raise them up. Next I remembered the adjoining bathroom and how I didn't like going in there.

"Search your feelings," John said. "See if you can remember the reason you don't like going in there."

"Because somebody's watching me all the time," I replied.

"Did you ever get up in the night to go to the bathroom?" John asked.

I nodded.

"Okay," John said. "Did you ever look out the window at night?"

"No. I didn't want to turn on the light."

"What would happen if you turned on the light?"

"I wasn't as much afraid if I didn't turn on the light."

"Hmm. All right. Okay. What are you thinking now?" John asked.

"I had to go to the kitchen to get some water."

"Picture yourself going to the kitchen," John instructed. "Is this night time?"

I nodded.

"Okay," John said. "Picture how dark it is in the house. Picture yourself fumbling and stumbling around trying to get there, being careful. Now, you arrive in the kitchen. Watch what you do."

I remembered feeling an urge to go outside and walking toward the door that led to the carport. "I want to go out the door," I explained.

"Why?" John asked.

"But, I don't know why."

"Well, let's watch and see what happens." After a long pause, John asked, "What happens next?"

The next thing I remembered was how incredibly quiet it was. I didn't remember walking out the door, but somehow I now stood in the back yard where I saw a beam of light and a spaceship. I felt compelled to go inside the spaceship. I suddenly found myself lying on a platform inside.

As I lay on the platform, several chalky-colored creatures with huge black eyes stood next to me. One turned its head to look at me. I noticed it had a long, thin neck. I lay still, calm and unafraid, as the creatures performed gynecological-type procedures on me. One creature, who seemed to be in charge, stood on the other side of the room and performed lab tests. I noticed the room was round and extremely bright, but I didn't recall seeing a source of the lighting.

"Does this feel like a dream?" John asked.

"The creatures were there," I replied matter-of-factly.

Then I remembered a creature did something to my right ear that caused pain in two places, directly behind the ear and inside it. I felt a piercing sensation as if something were being inserted. I remembered little else other than looking deeply into the creatures' eyes and feeling as if they were trying to comfort me.

"What's the next thing you remember after you were gone from that room?" John asked.

"I'm back in the kitchen."

"Okay. Did you just walk home, or how did you get in the kitchen?"

"I don't know."

"Okay. And what do you do now?"

"I get some water and go back to bed."

"That's a heck of a trip to the kitchen!" John remarked.

Since I could remember nothing further about that experience, John told me to concentrate on feeling as if I were suspended in some kind of light above my bed. He told me to visualize what house I lived in at the time and which bed that light was over.

"My bed in Craston," I replied.

John instructed me to go back a step in time and see what happened and where I was before I was suspended above my bed.

I remembered standing in a field and seeing a spaceship hovering in the air to the right of a large tree. I saw a beam of bright white light come toward me and envelope me. I was unable to move inside the light. I couldn't remember anything else about this experience.

"Then let your mind drift," John said, "and find what touched you to leave bruises."

"I keep seeing the creature," I replied.

"And where do you seem to be when you see this creature?"

"I don't know. He doesn't want me to know."

"He doesn't want you to know *what*?" John asked.

"He doesn't want me to remember," I answered.

"Does he do anything to keep you from remembering?"

"I don't know. He keeps looking at me with those eyes."

"You're not sure, are you?" John asked. "It all has to do with not remembering. When we talk about bruises, you see the creature. They didn't want you to remember how you got the bruises."

"No, they don't want me to remember."

Since I could remember nothing else, John pulled me out of hypnosis at that point.

"When did you have those ear problems?" John asked.

"Well, they didn't get bad until I moved to Craston. But the first time I had any problem with my ear was in Florence."

"When you were in Florence. Now, this time you remembered under hypnosis, was that in Florence?"

"Um-hum."

"Bingo!" John said. "And you said this pain was an allergy to copying machines, right?"

"Right." Everyone else in the room started laughing. "What are you laughing at?"

"I never heard of such a thing before," John answered. "The doctor you talked to had never heard of that."

"Well, that doesn't mean anything," I said. "Doctors don't know everything."

It was apparent John believed the pain I experienced in my right ear was the result of the aliens' procedure. I could tell I had failed in my attempts to convince him the problem resulted from copying machine ink.

Since we were at a standstill, John changed the subject. "You had a place in your back yard that was round and affected in some way. Now, which house was that?"

"I think it was Tuscaloosa, but I'm not sure," I answered.

"Well, describe the area—what happened to it, what it looked like," John requested.

"It was a perfectly round circle of brown, dead grass. The grass was green everywhere else."

"About how big around would you guess?" John asked.

I made a circle with my arms to indicate the size.

"Oh, about three feet in diameter?" John asked.

"Yeah, not real big," I replied.

"How long did it take for that circle to grow back?"

"It never did while we lived there."

"Well, what do you know!" John said. "Uh, don't you consider that a little strange?"

"Yeah, of course I do," I replied. "I always wondered what it was."

"We know she's not supposed to remember something," Seth added.

"Oh, yeah," John said. "But, in time, that may change. And it may leak out anyway in dreams again. 'Cause that's a point in time where we're at rest, where our defenses are down and what really is inside with our feelings and our thoughts often comes to the surface. If it was just a nice little dream, it would sound so much different than this stuff. 'Cause this stuff really, in a lot of ways, is boring. There's a real lack of creativity and diversity in these images. Especially when you get thousands of people who report the same exact thing—down to the skin color and the texture and the eyes. They always talk about the eyes over and over. And that's the main thing *you* always focus on—those eyes."

"It seems that the eye is *why* you don't remember," Grace explained. "Something about the eyes. It's like hypnosis."

"Yeah, it really is," John added. "Except they're not as nice as I am."

It had been a long session, and we all needed a break. We agreed to meet back at the office after dinner. John, keenly sensing I was too mentally taxed to undergo another hypnosis session, suggested we simply watch some videotapes that evening. I was having a hard time accepting the idea I had actually experienced the three alien encounters that had surfaced in the hypnosis sessions. Furthermore, I still refused to believe I really had been hypnotized. I thought my mind was playing tricks on me or else I was mentally ill. I sensed that John wanted me to see the videotapes so I would accept the reality of the abduction experiences and admit I had indeed been hypnotized.

The videotapes we watched that night were of two women who recalled abduction experiences under hypnosis. I was amazed. Their experiences were so similar to mine. The creatures they described were like the ones I had seen. The women had also seen a beam of light. Could this mean my experiences were real? Or did it simply mean there were several people who all had the same kind of mental illness? What if my experiences *were* real? I usually slept in nothing but panties and socks. Maybe, while practically naked, I had been seen by someone as I was being beamed aboard a spaceship. The thought embarrassed me. These thoughts and others churned around in my mind throughout the remainder of the evening and most of the night.

On Monday Seth and I met John for dinner after he got off work. I was too emotionally drained to eat. The three of us talked for a while. Then John told Seth and me that he had arranged for us to meet a woman named Paula who had been abducted by aliens many times. Here I was about to meet a real person who claimed to have seen extraterrestrial beings!

We arrived at the office before Paula did. As she walked into the room, she came toward me and gave me a big hug. I needed that. The gesture indicated she understood everything I was feeling.

Paula told me about her own encounters, but John had warned her previously not to tell me too much because he didn't want me to be "contaminated." He wanted to make sure what came out in any future hypnosis sessions was the result of my own memories and experiences and not something I had heard from someone else. That made sense. She did, however, tell me enough to convince me that she indeed had been abducted by aliens. Some of the experiences she shared resembled my own, and since the videotapes we had seen the night before also contained similar experiences, I began to believe my alien encounters were real. After all, here in front of me was a person who seemed normal in all respects. Someone who seemed honest and down-to-earth, yet extremely intelligent. And spiritual. That trait was important to me. I had wondered how the alien phenomenon fit into the concepts I had been taught through my Southern Baptist upbringing. More than once, the thought had occurred to me that maybe the aliens were really demons that had come to taunt me.

I listened to Paula's accounts with fascination. I could have listened all night. But the meeting had to come to an end at some point. It was time to say goodbye. Seth and I had to drive back home after breakfast the next morning, and I didn't know when I would see John, Grace, or Paula again. I didn't want to leave. Once I stepped outside that office I would have to face the new world alone. I didn't know if I could do it.

John must have sensed my fear of isolation. He suggested I write letters to him regularly. He explained there were two major reasons for that activity. First, it would be therapeutic for me to vent my frustrations on paper. Second, it would help John keep up with my experiences on a continuing basis and we wouldn't have to waste valuable time discussing them when I came back to Springfield for future sessions. After I promised John I would probably write more than he really wanted to read, John and Paula gave me a hug and said goodbye to Seth and me.

It was hard to hold back the tears. As we drove back to the inn, Seth commented he knew it would be hard for me to leave behind the support I had received in Springfield. Good old Seth. I silently thanked God that I had Seth with me right now.

47

CHAPTER FIVE

Tuesday, March 12, Seth and I drove back to Craston. We again sang along with Seth's Nitty Gritty Dirt Band tapes, but with less zeal. We were silent throughout much of the drive. I thought about what we had learned in Springfield, and I assumed Seth did, too.

We arrived in Craston late and Seth spent the night, leaving for home the next morning. During the remainder of the week, Kelly and Laura spent most of their time with friends, leaving me alone with my thoughts.

For days I wandered aimlessly about the house, accomplishing nothing. Before going to Springfield I had promised Mike I would prepare our income tax returns as soon as I returned. But now I was unable to concentrate on them. I knew I needed to pull myself together; however, I was unable to find either the energy or the motivation to do so. I felt almost as if I were in a state of shock.

Mike came home Friday night and asked if I had completed the returns. He wanted to know how much money we needed to borrow to pay the IRS. When I said I hadn't worked on the returns, he snapped at me. I immediately burst into tears and cried for hours until I finally fell asleep from exhaustion.

Saturday morning I felt much better but failed to understand why I had become so upset the night before. I would have had the right to be that upset if a family member or close friend had died or developed an incurable disease. But why be so upset about alien encounters? The creatures didn't want to frighten me; the medical procedures they performed seemed no worse than those performed by human doctors. So why fall apart when there was no reason for doing so?

I wasn't afraid the creatures might visit me again. On the contrary, I wanted them to come back. I remembered the comradeship I felt as a child when the creature calmed me, took my hand, and led me through the woods. I wondered where the creature was now. I wanted to learn more about these beings and the reasons for their mysterious visitations. I wanted to look into their eyes again and communicate with them. And I wanted to remember the experiences consciously.

But because so much had been blocked from conscious memory, I sometimes questioned the reality of the alien abductions. I told myself there could be other explanations. They could be hallucinations. They could be a symptom of mental illness. They could be an unusual type of dream. Or they could be a phenomenon of which I had no knowledge. But one thing I knew—the phenomenon was important enough to explore further. I could no longer brush it out of my mind and forget it.

Mike and I spent most of the weekend discussing these thoughts and the impact of the phenomenon on our family.

"How can we afford to continue this pursuit?" Mike asked. "Do you have any idea how long it will take to find your answers and how much it will cost? Don't you realize that in a year Laura will be in college and we still need to pay off our own college loans? And remember, in three years, we'll have two kids in college."

I told Mike I knew he was right but I had to continue exploring the subject. I also told him I felt as if I were being watched most of the time and I hoped no one had seen me being beamed out of the house wearing nothing but panties and socks.

Later that weekend Mike handed me a present. I looked at him quizzically, wondering why he was giving me a present when there was no occasion.

"Open it," he said. Inside were three lovely new nightgowns.

"I can't have my wife beamed through Craston inappropriately attired," Mike said.

It was good to find humor in a situation that was drastically changing our lives. We needed it to help us deal with the strange activities that were occurring.

Some of these activities were electrical in nature. After returning from Springfield, I had problems with long-distance phone calls. When Mike or I phoned each other, we heard static on the line and other phones ringing faintly in the background. When Mother phoned, she complained that my voice sounded as if it were coming from a deep hole, and we heard repetitive beeps on the line.

One day I phoned an abductee whom John suggested I contact. He felt I should hear about her experiences with people who appeared to be government agents. Shortly after we started talking, we heard an almost deafening click on the line followed by constant clicks as if someone were trying to disconnect us.

"Apparently someone doesn't want us to talk with each other," I said. "If we get cut off, I'll call you back on one of my other lines. If that doesn't work, I'll call you back soon from a pay phone." At that point, the annoying clicks stopped, and we heard nothing else on the line other than a slight hum.

Our security system continued to give us problems. It occasionally made odd, pinging noises at various times during the night. Sometimes the system was turned on when the sounds occurred; sometimes it was off. The security company could find no explanation for the malfunction.

On March 31, I spent several hours at the computer transcribing a tape of my hypnosis sessions. Before I saved my file, the power went off for a brief moment and I lost all my work. The next day I learned from neighbors that their electricity had not gone off at all.

I also began to hear beeps resembling Morse code when I lay down in bed at night. Hearing those sounds frustrated me because Mike claimed he couldn't hear them. I was unable to determine where they were coming from or why I heard them with only my right ear.

For several days, my right ear hurt badly in the same two places that had felt uncomfortable when the aliens had tampered with it. On March 29, my left ear began to hurt in the same two places as my right ear. Never having had any problems with my left ear before, I couldn't understand what caused the discomfort. On April 6, I woke up to find a spot of blood on my left ear.

Another puzzle was a phone conversation I had with my friend Judith. She called to learn the results of my trip to Springfield. I explained the hypnosis sessions revealed my alien encounters were real and apparently had started during childhood when I saw the spaceships in Gardendale. Judith gave no indication of surprise or disbelief, her calm reply indicating she readily accepted the reality of my encounters.

Then I told her that while in Springfield Seth and I discovered the government was actively but secretly investigating UFOs.

"*How* did you find *that* out!" Judith demanded.

I was shocked at Judith's sudden change in tone. Feeling I had somehow trespassed on sacred ground, I hastily changed the subject. But for reasons I couldn't understand, I felt a strain throughout the remainder of our conversation.

After we hung up, I thought about our conversation. I wondered why what I learned about our government's investigations into the UFO phenomenon upset Judith so much. Did she interpret my comment as a personal affront since her husband was in the Air Force? I wasn't sure; her reaction baffled me.

Another strange occurrence took place on Monday, March 18, my first day at work after spring break. I taught classes from nine o'clock until noon. Then I picked up a cheeseburger at a drive-through restaurant and drove back to the university so I could grade exams while I ate. As I returned to campus and parked my car, I noticed it was the only vehicle in sight. But, it was not unusual for the street to be deserted during lunch. I went to my office and started grading exams. After finishing my cheeseburger, I remembered I had left a business letter in the front seat of my car, and I decided to put it in the campus mail. I went to get it. Once outside, I saw a man looking in the front passenger window of my car.

"What is he doing?" I wondered.

I looked around to see if anything else looked suspicious. In a moment, the man saw me.

"What do I do?" I wondered. "He looks as if he's dressed too nicely to be a car thief. Should I approach him and ask him what he's doing? What if he has a gun? Should I call security?"

I didn't know what to do. I decided to take a chance and retrieve the letter as planned. When the man saw me approach my car, he stopped looking inside, walked around to the other side, and acted as if he were looking at something in the grass. All the while, he looked at me out of the corner of his eye. Likewise, I carefully watched him as I unlocked my car, climbed inside, and picked up the letter.

The letter was lying underneath another I had written to

John Carpenter. His address was facing upwards. I scanned the car to see if there was anything inside that would interest a passerby. A map of Missouri was the only other item visible.

With the doors locked, I sat in the car for several minutes and glanced at the stranger. I noticed the man was still watching me. All of a sudden I noticed a pickup truck parked in front of my car. I realized it must belong to that man. I immediately memorized the number on the license plate. As I concentrated on it, the man quickly walked to the truck, threw a long, thin tool in the back, climbed inside, and sped off.

I puzzled over the situation. Maybe the man *was* merely interested in something in the grass, but why had he been looking in the window of my car? And what did he intend to do with that long, thin tool?

While studying the license plate, I had noticed there was no university parking decal on the truck; the vehicle apparently did not belong to a faculty or staff member or a student. Besides, since the university is small, I knew almost all of them. But I had never seen that man before.

I got a good look at him. He had short hair and a lean but strong-looking build. He wore gray slacks, a blue oxford-cloth shirt, and a tie.

The next day I stopped at the courthouse to see if I could obtain any information concerning the owner of the vehicle. I was able to get his name and address. The vehicle was registered to a man who lived in a town that was unfamiliar to me. When I got home, I located it on the map. It was approximately 250 miles from Craston. I wondered why a man who lived so far away was snooping around my car. Then I noticed on the map that his hometown was located near a NASA test site. I couldn't help but wonder whether this man worked there.

My memory raced to the night the men watched my family in a restaurant and then to the day in my office when I thought the young man was going to rape me. These men had the same traits as the man who was interested in my car: short hair, lean bodies, attractive clothing—traits that didn't belong to the typical Craston male. Could there be a connection between these men?

Several days later Mike came home from work and told me an employee whispered to him that she didn't know if it was in the best interest of the company to have him working there if he was being investigated by the FBI. We wondered why the FBI was investigating Mike when he hadn't been involved in any questionable activities. We could think of no reason other than my recent interest in extraterrestrials.

I began to be increasingly disturbed by the puzzling events, and I hoped they would stop. They didn't.

Throughout the spring semester, I had been teaching an accounting class on Monday evenings at the Air Force base. Immediately after class on April 29, Ginger Pugh (pseudonym), an older student, approached my desk and handed me something. "My husband said to give this to you."

"What is it?" I asked her.

"A patch of the space shuttle *Endeavour*."

"Oh," I said, looking at it. "Uh, why did your husband send this to me?"

"I don't know," she replied. "He just asked me to give it to you."

"Okay," I said. "Tell him I said thanks."

I didn't know Ginger's husband. I wasn't certain if I had ever met him. Why did he send me this patch?

When I got home, I looked on the class phone list for Ginger's number and dialed it. I didn't know what to say to her husband when he answered, so I got straight to the point. I said I called to thank him for the patch but I wondered why he sent it to me. He said Ginger had enjoyed my class so much that he wanted to give me a token of their appreciation.

"Bullshit!" I thought.

He added that as a further indication of their thanks, he would like to take me to see the space shuttle when it came to the Air Force base. And I could take pictures of it! He said he'd give me a call when the next shuttle arrived.

Not knowing what to say, I merely thanked him again and hung up. I was suspicious of his intentions. I did not believe his wife enjoyed my accounting class that much. She was struggling to get a C. Furthermore, if she did enjoy my class that much, why didn't she give me a gift herself? And why did the gift pertain to space? I concluded the patch was some sort of message, but I didn't understand what it meant or under whose orders it was sent.

Captain Pugh phoned Sunday night, May 5, and invited me to view the new space shuttle *Endeavour* which was scheduled to land on base the next day. He stressed the importance of not telling anyone I was going because the invitation was extended to me alone. Several times he told me to be sure to bring along my camera so I could take pictures.

"Why am I being issued a special invitation such as this?" I thought. "And why will I be allowed to take all the pictures I want? I'm a simple person, a mere accounting instructor, a nobody. There's something fishy going on here."

I felt it would be a mistake for me to go with Captain Pugh alone, but I didn't want him to know I was suspicious of his motives. I told him I would love to see the shuttle but I would be tied up all day Monday giving final exams. He replied he could take me Tuesday morning before the shuttle left for Florida. I told him I would have to check my appointment book and I would call him back Monday night after class to let him know whether I was free on Tuesday morning.

His persistence disturbed me. It was clear he was disappointed I wouldn't make a commitment to go with him to see the *Endeavour*.

My schedule Monday was hectic, but Judith persuaded me to take a break and meet her for lunch. Although I did not go into detail, I mentioned I was upset over the Air Force's obvious interest in me. Judith became defensive. She insisted the Air Force had ceased investigation of UFOs with Project Blue Book. I told her I knew otherwise. We argued about the subject. I left the restaurant upset that Judith refused to believe me.

During the afternoon, I started feeling drowsy and weak, thankful I was administering exams that day instead of lecturing. Yet, because of my conversations with Captain Pugh, I dreaded going out to the base that night to administer the final exam to that class.

Before I went, I took a few precautions just in case the Air Force tried anything. I emptied my purse of everything other than my driver's license and keys. I dumped out my aspirin and antihistamines so I wouldn't give the military an excuse to question me concerning drug possession. Then I hitched a ride with one of my students because I didn't want to be accused of driving violations.

While my students were taking their exams, I read a magazine. Occasionally, I looked up to make sure they were not letting their eyes wander to someone else's paper. The last time I looked up, I saw a man in a blue uniform standing in the hall motioning for me to come outside.

"Oh, God!" I thought. "What does that man want?"

I walked out of the classroom and noticed the man was an Air Force officer. He had what appeared to be a two-way radio attached to his belt and the name "Pugh" on his shirt.

"Let's go," he said without greeting. "Let's go look at it right now."

"Look at what?" I asked.

"You know, the shuttle. Let's go look at it."

"I can't leave my students while they're taking their exams."

"Sure you can," he argued. "They won't care."

"No, I can't," I said. "Look, I think it's really nice of you to want to take me on a private tour of the shuttle. But I can't go right now. I can't leave my students."

"They won't care," he said again.

"I would really like to go, but I would get fired if I were to desert my students," I told him.

"It'll only take about twenty minutes," he continued to argue. "Besides, your students won't tell on you. They won't care."

"I really do appreciate your offer," I said, "but I'm going to have to take a rain check. I know the shuttles land here frequently, so I'll take you up on your offer some other time. I don't want to risk getting fired."

"How about tomorrow morning?" he asked, obviously not giving up. "The shuttle's supposed to take off at 6:00, but I can arrange for you to see it before it leaves. And be sure to bring your camera so you can get some good pictures of it."

"I have painters coming to my house tomorrow morning," I explained. "I have to be there." I didn't want to lie. I did have painters coming over the next morning, but I knew they wouldn't be there before 7:00.

"Well, I'll be back in an hour or so after your students have had time to finish their exams, and I'll take you then," he said.

"I can't go after the exam because I rode with someone," I explained.

"Well, that person can come, too," he said.

"And how are you going to get rid of him?" I thought. But instead I said, "He needs to get back home right after class. I can't delay him. I really do appreciate, though, your going to all this trouble to set things up." I wondered if he caught my pun about a setup.

It seemed he didn't. "Well, it really wasn't too much trouble," he replied. "I knew you'd be interested in seeing the shuttle since you're writing a book about space phenomena."

I wasn't writing a book about anything at that time, but I remembered the excuse I gave students and colleagues concerning the nature of my trip to Springfield over spring break. "What makes you think the book I intend to write has anything to do with this sort of stuff?" I asked.

"Ginger said that you told some students you intended to write a book about space phenomena and that the government didn't want the public to know much about that subject."

"I haven't told any student anything about the particular subject matter of my book!" I emphasized.

I wondered what this man was up to. Mike and Judith were still the only people in Craston with whom I had discussed UFOs.

"Well, you seemed really interested in the patch I sent you," Captain Pugh replied, trying a new approach.

"Yes, thanks again," I said. "I've always been interested in space travel. Well, I've got to go back into the classroom in case a student has a question about the exam. I'll have to see the shuttle some other time."

I went back into the classroom and pondered our conversation. Was Pugh's mention of the subject matter of my research a slipup, or did he make that statement intentionally?

What was he after? I had noticed his nervousness as we talked. He kept shifting from one foot to the other and wringing his hands. I wondered what would have happened to me if I had gone with him. It occurred to me he didn't care if I lost my job. It angered me he would try to put my job in jeopardy like that.

As soon as I got home, I phoned Captain Pugh to get a better idea why he wanted me to view the shuttle. He put me on hold for a long time before talking with me. I wondered what he was doing for such a long time. Why didn't he simply call me back if he was busy right then?

Finally he picked up the phone again, and I explained why I was calling. "Captain Pugh, I want to thank you again for your invitation, but I want you to understand I couldn't leave my class like that."

"Yeah, I understand," he replied. "Anyway, I found out the *Discovery* is going to be here around the end of this week. I know you'll be finished with all your exams by then, so you'll have enough free time to go look at it. And be sure to bring your camera along. You'll be able to get some good pictures of it."

"Okay. I'll do that. But I'm curious about something. What exactly did Ginger say about the subject matter of my book?"

"I don't know what you're talking about," he said with a tone that sounded agitated.

"You said earlier this evening that Ginger said I told some of my students I intend to write a book about space phenomena."

"I didn't say any such thing!" he retorted.

"Yes, you did," I insisted. "Remember? You said Ginger told you I intend to write a book about space phenomena and the government doesn't want the public to know very much about it."

"I never said any such thing," he snapped back.

"Well, okay. I must have misunderstood," I said. But I knew I hadn't misunderstood. So why did Pugh adamantly deny his statement now? Was our conversation being monitored?

I decided to say something for the record just in case it was. "I just want you to know that none of my students know the particular subject matter I'm researching. No one could possibly know that unless they've got my phones tapped or unless they've been in my house reading my notes."

Captain Pugh changed the subject. He talked at length about how he would like to teach some evening courses at the university where I worked. He ended our conversation with the promise to call me when the next space shuttle came to Craston.

The next day an article in the local paper emphasized that security guards posted around the *Endeavour* during its visit carried automatic weapons and were authorized to use deadly force. The words made me shudder. I couldn't help but wonder if the deadly force was meant for me and if my corresponding obituary should have been on another page of the paper. I was very glad I had not accepted Captain Pugh's invitation, and I hoped he would never contact me again.

On May 10, I obtained some additional information about the man I caught snooping around my car on March 18. He worked in the metrology lab for a division of NASA which was responsible for calibrating the equipment associated with the space shuttles' external tanks. Hardly a car thief, it seemed!

This new information coupled with the Air Force's superficial invitation to view the *Endeavour* terrified me. But it also aroused my curiosity. Why was I attracting so much government and military interest? If there was something about my involvement with the creatures that would attract the attention of these agencies, then it must be very important. And despite my fear, I intended to get to the bottom of it.

CHAPTER SIX

While Seth and I were in Springfield for my first set of hypnosis sessions, John Carpenter told me not to be surprised if memories of prior experiences started creeping into my consciousness. He explained hypnotic regression sometimes triggers memories that have been buried. I found this to be true. I immediately started having flashbacks related to my prior alien encounters. Sometimes these flashbacks were fleeting memories of one tiny portion of my experiences. Sometimes the flashbacks were longer in duration and brought back larger chunks of experiences.

I remembered the color and sizes of the test tubes the aliens used and the maneuvers of the spaceships I saw in Gardendale before two of them whizzed away. I remembered a beam of light coming from the bottom of another spaceship. I remembered being at an unknown location and replacing the mouthpiece my dentist required me to wear at night. What disturbed me most about these memories was knowing much more remained that I could not remember.

My conference room dream of late January or early February crossed my mind frequently. I knew there was something very important about that conference room, but I couldn't remember what.

Some of my memories were extremely unpleasant. I began to get indications that my dream of having sex with a spirit was not a dream at all. At first I remembered only that the entity had a physical form and was extremely ugly. Later I saw flashes of a creature that resembled a gremlin, but it was much taller and thinner. I couldn't recall its color, yet I knew it was one of the ugliest things imaginable.

One flashback occurred when Mike was home, shortly after we went to bed. Mike had left a light on in the bathroom, allowing a sliver of light to shine into our bedroom. Mike turned to face me. All of a sudden he turned his head in such a way that the light sent a glare across his eyes. I

61

cringed, started trembling, pulled away, and broke into tears. I didn't understand exactly why it happened. But when the glare shone in Mike's eyes, for one brief moment, I could see myself experiencing something dreadful and terrifying. And I knew it involved a creature. Then, as suddenly as the memory raced across my mind, it was gone.

Mike was very understanding. He held me close and listened patiently as I tried to explain what had raced through my head. But it was hard to explain since I didn't understand it myself.

Not only did I begin to recall portions of my experiences, I began to have additional lucid dreams about aliens and spaceships.

One occurred during the night of March 29, 1991. I woke up at approximately 3:00 a.m. and saw a bright light shining through my bedroom window. I was too tired to get up to see what it was. I told myself it was probably brightness from the moon, but if the light emanated from a spaceship instead, the aliens could come on in and get me. I was ready for them. But I soon fell asleep and dreamed the aliens put Mike in a trance. They tried to do the same with me, but I fought against their powers because I wanted to remember everything. The aliens had a different idea, however. They floated a green sphere into the room to control me.

Two nights later I dreamed I was pulled out of bed by a great force, like that of a powerful magnet or giant vacuum. I sped through the air and ended up in what I first thought was a spaceship that was whirling around. When the whirling stopped, I found myself standing in a room decorated with antiques. Spotting a telephone on a table, I told myself the room could not be part of a spaceship. But then an alien took my hand, led me to another room, and made me lie down. I could see nothing clearly in this room; it looked as if it were filled with dense mist or fog. I could barely see the forms of several creatures moving about. They began to perform painful gynecological procedures on me. I screamed out for them to stop. An alien told me it would be okay, that I wouldn't remember anything. Then I lost consciousness. Later I found myself back at home, but not in my bed. Feeling groggy, I was unable to determine exactly where I was. It seemed I was in Kelly's bedroom or in the hall just outside it.

The next morning I woke up in my own bed.

Upon awakening, I felt a burning irritation inside my vaginal area. I blamed the problem on the hot pepper sauce and jelly beans I had eaten the day before. I decided to avoid those foods in the future, hoping to prevent such physical discomfort and distressful dreams.

But I could not deny the feeling that portions of both dreams were more real than dreamlike. I decided if aliens truly did exist, then I probably was abducted while I was asleep those two nights.

Although I had always believed extraterrestrials existed and probably visited Earth, I had never thought they would visit *me*. Why did they? Was it because I happened to be outside playing that day in Gardendale? Did they look down from the sky at that moment and say, "Hey, there are a few kids down there; let's go get one"? Did they somehow make us go looking for them in the woods? Why did they pick me? Why not Seth or Philip or Mr. Goode? Was it because I was the one who ventured out in the direction of their spaceship?

I wanted answers to these questions. I wanted to know why I had attracted the attention of NASA and the Air Force. I decided to go back to Springfield for additional hypnosis sessions at the first opportunity.

CHAPTER SEVEN

I flew to Springfield on May 16, 1991. Since I now felt comfortable with John and Grace, I did not need to bring anyone along this time for moral support.

Upon arriving at the airport, I called the hotel and asked the clerk to send their van to pick me up. The clerk replied someone had already called and the van was on its way. I walked to the door where the clerk told me to wait and noticed a man standing there alone.

"Are you waiting for the hotel van?" I asked.

"Yes," he replied.

To pass the time, I initiated a conversation with this stranger. I asked him where he was from and what brought him to Springfield. He told me he was a salesman from Nashville and was in Springfield to interview for a position at a sporting goods store.

"What brings *you* here?" he asked.

"I'm here to do research concerning some personal experiences."

"About extraterrestrials?" he asked.

I was stunned. Why would a stranger ask if my research involved extraterrestrials?

"Yeah, you're right," I replied. "But how did you know that? Who do you work for? The CIA? FBI? NSA? MJ-12?"

"I told you. I'm a salesman from Nashville."

"Yeah. I know what you told me."

I didn't know how to deal with this situation. I felt uneasy about getting on the van with a man I suspected of being a government agent. Yet, I knew if a government agency planned to eliminate me, it would ultimately accomplish its task regardless of whether or not I got on the van with this man. And my suspicions could be wrong. There was a slight possibility the man truly was a salesman from Nashville who guessed the subject matter of my research by chance.

During the ride to the hotel I discussed only things about

myself government agents would already know if they were keeping a file on me: places I had lived, my occupation, my fondness of fishing.

"Tell me about your UFO experiences," he finally said.

"I'm more interested in knowing whether *you've* ever encountered a UFO," I replied.

He told me a story about shooting a BB gun at a UFO when he was a child.

"That sounds like bullshit," I thought, but instead I replied, "Oh, that's really interesting."

We soon arrived at the hotel, checked in, and went our separate ways. I never saw the man again.

John, Grace, and I met the next evening in my hotel suite for my third hypnosis session. We decided to explore the dream in which I was pulled out of bed by a powerful force and found myself in a room filled with antiques. After we went through the relaxation process, John asked me to think about the events that occurred during the evening of March 31, 1991, prior to this dream.

I described how annoyed I was when the power blinked off for a moment, causing me to lose the work I had done on the computer. I remembered that soon afterwards the office telephone rang, but when I answered it, I heard nothing but breathing. Disturbed by the phone call, I went to bed and read before falling asleep.

"What's the very first thing you notice as you start to sleep?" John asked. "Be aware of your bed and where you are. You start having a dream that you consciously remembered. How did that dream begin?"

"I was awakened by some kind of force jerking me out of bed. I don't see the force clearly. I'm moving too fast."

I realized I was remembering a real event, not a dream.

"Is there any color to the force?" John asked.

"It's similar to the color of fog."

"So, is that white and misty?"

"Yes," I replied.

"What illuminates the fog?"

"I'm not sure."

"Feel yourself now in the energy that you call a force. Feel it and describe what you notice."

"I'm moving back and forth within its boundaries," I explained. "I'm basically lying down, but my arms and legs are moving around."

"Do you actually bounce off one side and the other like you're in something?" John asked.

"I don't ever feel as if I'm hitting a side of anything."

"Follow the energy force you feel yourself in, and see where you go next," John instructed.

"I think I'm in a spaceship in the air."

"What helps you decide that you may be on a spaceship? Why wouldn't you be at the corner grocery or in a hotel room? What makes the difference that leads you to believe that you're in a spaceship in the air?"

"I saw it, but I..."

"From the outside?" John interrupted.

"Yes. It seems that at one point I'm standing on the ground looking up at it; at another point I'm off the ground looking at it. But that's not possible."

"Oh, I realize that," John said. "And if you are off the ground, perhaps you're standing on some kind of elevator or something."

"No. It's like I'm suspended," I replied.

"What do you see in that perception of being suspended?"

"A big, round silver object."

"And have you ever seen anything like that before?" John asked.

"Yes."

"How close does it seem?"

"It's close enough that I can touch it if I want to."

"Are you alone?"

"Yes."

"What's the next part that you recall?"

I described the dizzy sensation I felt as the spaceship spun through the air. When the spinning stopped, I found myself in a round room occupied by the same creatures I had seen before. I watched them as they adjusted their equipment. I lay down on a table as they moved the equipment toward me. When I looked up, I saw a large piece of medical equipment extending above my head. A creature stood next to my right side; I felt at peace as I gazed into its eyes. A bright light almost blinded me, but I couldn't see the source of the lighting.

"So what happens now?" John asked.

"They're scraping samples from the vaginal area. They're using some kind of metal object."

"Feel any sensations that go with that," John directed. "But you only have to feel them for a moment, just in order to remember."

"Now I feel pain in my right ovary. A severe pain in my right ovary."

The pain finally ceased as I caught a glimpse of an object that aroused my curiosity. "I'm wondering what that box-like thing is," I said. "A creature's holding it in its hand."

"What color is the box?" John asked.

"Black."

"What does he do with it?"

"I don't remember anything else. I'm back in my house, sitting on the floor. I think I'm in the hall outside Kelly's room."

"So what do you do next after you come to sitting on the floor?"

"I just walk down the hall and go back to bed," I explained.

At that point, John brought me out of hypnosis. Again I denied being hypnotized and argued that I must have a distorted mind that was making up lies.

"Well, I can tell you're awake again," John said. "Any time I ask you while you're under, you go, 'Oh, it's real.' And then when you come out, you go, 'Oh, no, it's a lie; I made it all up.' Under hypnosis, you really believe your sensations are genuine, but when you come out, all the doubt and judgment and criticism come back in because it just doesn't fit with your everyday experiences."

John was right, of course. I knew the experiences were real. But it was difficult to accept this new expanded view of reality.

"Did one of you turn on a light?" I asked.

"No," both John and Grace replied.

"Neither of you turned on a light?" I asked again.

"We didn't get up," Grace said.

"We didn't move," John agreed.

"There was a light that was so bright that it blinded me," I said. "I thought you guys had turned the light on."

"Oh, no," John emphasized. "I remember that you covered your eyes at one point."

If I had not trusted John and Grace completely, I would have sworn that they flashed a bright light in my face during the session. But they said they didn't, and I believed them.

"What does this memory have to do with the room filled with antiques?" I wanted to know.

"Your dream may have been a dream that incorporated a real experience," John explained.

"That means the little visitors came to my new house," I mused.

"Yep," John agreed. "Of course, that was the night the power went off only in your house and you woke up with a physical irritation," he added as he pulled out the letter I had written him concerning these events. "You've documented the exact date."

John and Grace left me with these thoughts to mull over until our next session the following night.

The next night John decided to explore the dream I had in late January or early February, 1991. Before we began hypnosis, John asked me to summarize the dream for him and Grace again.

I briefly reiterated that in one scene I was suspended above my bed, in another I was standing outside looking at the night sky and thinking I needed to get back inside, and in the third I was sitting in a conference room talking about UFOs.

I recently had remembered more details about the third scene and had indicated to John that I was quite disturbed by them. I recalled men seated around the conference room table. I was wearing a man's coat and answering questions about UFOs while seated at one end of the table. I also remembered a woman who wore a blue uniform. This memory had been haunting me for some inexplicable reason since my trip to Springfield in March.

As soon as John, Grace, and I discussed this dream, John began hypnosis. After completing the relaxation process, John asked me to remember a time in Craston when I was standing in my back yard at night.

"It's not my yard," I hastily replied. "I don't know where I am. It's like a clearing. I don't know what I'm doing out there all alone. There are a lot of trees in the background."

"What time of night does it seem to be?" John asked.

"There are stars in the sky."

"What are you wearing?"

"I don't remember."

"Okay. What happens next?"

"I don't think this can happen!" I said, becoming quite agitated, not wanting to remember the scene taking place in front of me.

"Well, tell us what you *think* is happening," John insisted. "You don't have to understand it. Just report what you see happening."

"There are people with guns," I said. "They're in the clearing. They're getting out of a helicopter or something."

"All right. Take a good close look at the helicopter or something. What do you see?"

"It *is* a helicopter! People are getting out of it. They've got weapons. Big machine-gun-like weapons. They're wearing green uniforms."

"Any hats?" John asked.

"There's one with a hat, but he doesn't have on the green uniform. He has on a blue hat, shirt, and pants."

"What are you doing?" John wanted to know.

"They're making me get in the helicopter."

"But you must fight them and try to run away, don't you?" John asked.

"No. I'm afraid of their guns!" I explained.

"What did you hear that made you know you had to go with them?"

"I don't remember them saying anything," I answered. "They just came out of the helicopter, grabbed me, and shoved me inside."

"So is there anyone else with you besides the men with the guns?"

"No," I replied. "The man with the blue shirt seems to be in charge. He said I'm a troublemaker and they're going to shut me up. They have me sitting down on the floor of the helicopter. It's cold and hard. The men are sitting around me with guns."

"Did they keep the guns pointed at you?" John asked.

"I don't remember that. I said something to the man in charge, and they got mad and shoved me down."

"What did you say to him?"

"I told him he was an asshole and I wasn't going to let him shut me up."

"Now maybe you notice what you're wearing as you feel the cold, hard floor of the helicopter," John said.

"There's nothing on my arms," I remarked. "The men grabbed me by my arms on both sides. I told them to get their nasty hands off me, but they just kept on grabbing me."

"Did they do anything to hurt you?" John asked.

"I was struggling with them as I was coming off the helicopter. I don't understand why they're taking me there." I felt a sudden chill. "It's cold," I remarked. "There's a man on each side of me holding my arms tightly. They're taking me into a building."

"Now you can see the door open," John directed, "and you can catch a glimpse right away of what's inside."

"I'm looking at the people in there." I saw men seated along the left side of the conference room table. The man in the blue uniform was standing to my right. A man decorated with military pins was standing at the opposite end of the table.

"What do you notice right now?" John asked.

"Somebody's giving me a shot in my right arm. It feels like a tetanus shot."

"Don't you fight and scream?" John wondered.

"The guys in the uniforms are still holding me tightly," I explained.

"What do they look like? You must be able to see them a little more clearly now. Do they have long hair and bushy eyebrows or..."

"No," I interrupted. "No. They look like military people. Real short hair."

"See clearly now," John instructed. "See if any of them look familiar."

"They don't look familiar."

"That's fine. Notice exactly where you are at this moment...whether you're standing there..."

"I was standing there when they gave me a shot, but then they shoved me into a chair."

"What do you seem to notice after you're shoved into the seat?" John asked.

"I'm just feeling dizzy."

"So you're sitting on the chair, feeling a little dizzy. Look around you now as you sit there, and notice what your attention is drawn to. What do you focus on?"

"I can't. I'm feeling too dizzy," I explained.

"All right," John said. "What do you hear? Listen carefully. There must be some kind of talking or interaction with somebody somewhere. Or is it totally silent?"

"The man who was in the helicopter said something first. He said, 'Here she is. She's a cocky little bitch.' Then somebody on the other side of the room said, 'Well, we'll just take care of that!'"

"And then what do you hear?"

"I don't remember. It's cold in there."

"Why is it cold for you? Don't you have on your coat?"

"I'm not cold any more," I replied.

"And how is it that you're not cold any more?" John asked.

"Somebody came up from behind me and put a jacket around my shoulders."

"Does the jacket touch the rest of your clothes?"

"I don't think I had anything else on except maybe some panties, but I...I must have had some clothes on!"

"What do you hear now?" John asked.

"There's a man talking to me. He's telling me I haven't seen anything. He's not very nice."

"How is he not nice?" John asked.

"His tone of voice," I replied.

"Do you see him or do you just hear him?"

"I don't see him because I'm so dizzy. I'm leaning my head over."

"Where is he standing in relation to you when you hear the voice?"

"At first he was on the other side of the room, but then he comes close to me and sort of props himself up against the table."

"What else does he say?" John asked.

"He said, 'You didn't see a spaceship. Do you understand? You did *not* see a spaceship.' I told him that I knew it was a spaceship and I didn't care what he said. I knew what it was."

"And how did he react to that statement of yours?"

"He said to the man in blue, 'Yeah, I see what you mean.'

Then I told them the only way they're going to shut me up is to kill me."

"Say that again!" John said, raising his voice.

"I told them the only way they're going to shut me up is to kill me," I repeated.

"How do they react to that statement?" John questioned.

"He said if I didn't cooperate, if it was necessary, that's exactly what they'd do."

"How do you feel when you hear that?" John wondered.

"It makes me angry."

"And how does it make them feel to say it?"

"They're angry, too."

"And now what is said?" John asked.

"I told him I didn't care if they killed me. I asked him what they wanted from me. I said, 'I haven't done anything. What do you want from me?'"

"Um-hum," John said. "What do you hear?"

"He said, 'Shut up and listen!'"

"So what do you listen to?" John asked.

"I told him I wasn't ready to shut up. I asked him what he was trying to cover up."

"Um-hum. And?"

"He said, 'It's none of your damned business. Just shut up and listen!'"

"So what do they try to tell you then if they want you to shut up and listen?"

"He told me that I hadn't seen anything and I didn't know anything."

"And that's what you're supposed to remember?" John paused. "So this is a nice dream that you're having?"

"No! I know I'm there, and I know the people are there. That man was real. And he wasn't very nice."

"Okay," John said. "So how does it end up?"

"There was a lady in the room for just a minute. She brought in a tape recorder. She laid it on the end of the table at the other end of the room."

"What do they do with that?" John asked.

"I don't know what they did with it after I got dizzy. I just remember her setting it on the table and leaving the room. She has on a blue uniform like the man who brought me in."

I could remember nothing more of significance, so John

brought me out of the trance. After spending a long time talking with me about the possible motives of the men who had captured me, John and Grace had to leave.

The hypnosis session was the most upsetting one I had undergone. All sorts of thoughts leaped into my mind. Now it seemed probable the man I had met at the airport *was* a government agent. What if I was being monitored closely while in Springfield? We had just finished a hypnosis session in my hotel suite. What if my room was bugged? "Oh, my God," I thought, "after remembering what I just did, I might be silenced tonight!" Although it was almost 1:30 a.m., I decided to take a shower. I wanted to be clean when I died.

Too upset to sleep, I climbed into bed and continued to think about my strange hypnosis session. To me, nothing could justify the treatment I had received from the men who had abducted me. I could excuse the abductions by the alien creatures by telling myself that since they were different, perhaps they didn't understand the pain and trauma they caused their human subjects. But these fellow human beings certainly understood; they knew exactly how I felt. They simply didn't care.

I could usually find comfort by reading the Bible, so I picked up the hotel copy and turned to the twenty-third Psalm. I read it over and over. Then I began to pray. I asked God what the alien phenomenon was all about. Were the aliens I had encountered good or evil? What was their relationship with God, with me, with each other? Why was a faction of our military and government trying to cover up the aliens' existence? I begged God to answer these questions because I was trying so hard to understand.

While praying, I began to see images flashing through my mind as if they were being scrolled on a computer screen: a fish, a four-pointed star, a sickle, a swastika, a wagon wheel, the side view of a dove, and all kinds of angels. I saw other images I couldn't remember afterwards because they flashed through my mind too quickly.

Now I was more confused than ever. I had never experienced anything like that. Why did I see symbols in my mind? What was happening to me? Was I losing the last bit of my sanity? Or was God trying to give me some kind of a message in answer to my prayers? If so, why didn't He do so in a direct manner? Didn't He understand how stupid I was and that I would not understand the symbols? I needed Him to spell things out for me.

Despite the added confusion after seeing the symbols, I felt a message of peace in them and eventually was able to fall asleep.

CHAPTER EIGHT

The next morning the sound of a man's voice in the adjacent room awakened me. The voice sounded vaguely familiar, so I put my ear to the wall and strained to hear what he was saying. I listened for what seemed like a long time, but I was able to make out only a few words dispersed throughout the conversation: "Memory implant...I tried several times, but...About places she lived...Craston, Tuscaloosa...Will do...Well, we got most of it...Four digits... U. S. government...I have served you well."

Hearing only one voice, I assumed the man was talking to someone over the phone. It finally occurred to me the voice sounded like that of the "salesman from Nashville" I had met at the airport. He mentioned Craston and Tuscaloosa, places I had lived, so I concluded the conversation was about me.

I became very frightened. I jumped out of bed, threw on some clothes, grabbed my purse, and ran downstairs to the lobby. I called Grace from a pay phone and told her what I had overheard. I felt someone should know what was going on in case something happened to me.

Grace contacted John who soon phoned to make sure I would not be alone during the day. I told him I had made arrangements to spend the day with an abductee he had told me to call and that she would be arriving at the hotel shortly. John described her appearance, told me to meet her at a specific location in the lobby, and warned me not to talk with anyone else. As if I needed any warning—I was terrified!

While waiting for my companion to arrive, I thought about the words I had overheard earlier. I wondered what a memory implant was. I interpreted the phrase "we got most of it" to mean the man had succeeded in recording most of my last two hypnosis sessions. The words "I have served you well" seemed to indicate that someone had hired this man to bug my room. But who? Sadly, I knew I probably would never know.

To my relief, the remainder of the day passed without any problems, and I met John and Grace that evening as planned for my fifth hypnosis session. We decided not to conduct the session in my hotel room this time.

The first experience John decided to explore that night was what happened to me before I found myself in the clearing surrounded by men with machine guns.

Under hypnosis, my first memory was being in a white beam of light. Then I saw the familiar eyes of the chalky-colored creatures and several lights swinging back and forth methodically as I lay on the familiar platform. After a while, only one blindingly bright light shone in my eyes. When the light left, I saw an oddly shaped piece of equipment over my abdomen. A long needle-like object entered my body. I felt a severe pain in my right ovary and pressure all the way to my back. I wanted it to stop. It finally did. Then a creature on my left began to examine the skin on my abdomen and thighs. I wondered why he kept moving my skin with his hands and feeling the bones underneath.

The touch of the creature's hands felt like rubber gloves. As he examined me, I noticed his hands were a bone color and had only four long, skinny fingers.

When he finished looking at my skin, he scraped tissue samples from the vaginal area. A creature standing to my right comforted me throughout these procedures.

"How does he comfort you?" John asked.

"With his eyes," I explained. "It's the big black eyes like I've seen before."

"But that would scare me. How do they comfort you?" John wanted to know.

"I've seen those eyes many times before. They've comforted me many times," I said, feeling calm and relaxed as I saw them.

"How long ago can you remember those eyes?" John asked. "Think back, way back to the first time you can remember those eyes. The very first time. Drift through time and find the first time you ever saw the eyes."

I drifted back to when I was three years old, playing with Seth in sandy soil at the edge of an Alabama lake. Our parents sat nearby on the bank and watched us. I glanced up and saw the odd-looking creature with the big black eyes.

"It was a cute little thing," I finally said to John.

"Where did you catch sight of this cute little thing?" John asked.

"My brother and I were playing with it. We were at the edge of the woods. My brother had on diapers."

"Where did the little thing come from?" John asked.

"It was inside the woods, near the edge, when I saw it," I explained. "Seth and I were next to the woods."

"Uh-huh. And why didn't you run at the sight of it?" John wondered.

"Because it was cute."

"And what made it cute?" John wanted to know.

"It had real big funny eyes," I replied.

"Perhaps you can remember your first reactions and what you thought maybe it was when you first saw it."

"I just think it's some other kind of little cute kid, but different from us. Another kind."

"Did it smile at you and giggle and laugh with you?" John asked.

"No," I replied. "It just kept turning its head in a funny way. Its head was so big I thought it was going to fall off."

"So, was it taller than you?"

"Yeah. It was a lot taller."

"What did your brother do with it?" John inquired.

"He gave it a rock," I answered. "My brother gave everybody rocks."

"What did the creature do with the rock?"

"It turned its head and looked with those eyes like it was pleased to have it."

"Did it smile?" John asked.

"It didn't have a mouth," I remarked.

"How did it show that it was pleased?" John wondered.

"It's the eyes and the way it was moving its head. I could just tell."

"So, did it show you anything in return?"

"The creature takes my hand, and I take my brother's hand. We go through the woods." I paused for a few seconds. "I don't think we should go. Mother's going to get real mad."

"And what does it tell you?"

"It can't talk. But I understand it," I explained. "It tells me that it'll make things okay with my mother."

"And how do you know that if it doesn't talk?" John asked.

"With its eyes."

"Okay. And then what happens?"

"It points to a big ball in the sky and asks if we want to go for a ride," I said.

"And what does the big ball in the sky look like?"

"It's round and silver and shiny. It's just sitting in the air."

"And what do you want to do?"

"I want to go for a ride."

"Oh, boy!" John exclaimed, as if he were talking to a child. "That would be fun! What happens now?"

"The creature tells us that we're going to step in a thing sort of like an elevator."

"So notice what you see that may be this elevator-like thing," John requested.

"It's like a light beam," I said. "I hadn't seen anything like it before; it looked real neat. The creature says, 'Just step in it and we'll go to the spaceship.' And we all get in it and join hands like we're going to play Ring Around the Rosy."

"What happens next?" John asked.

"We go to that round ball."

"What do you see as you go up?"

"Can't see anything."

The next thing I remembered was being inside the craft.

"Are there other kids there?" John asked.

"No. Just other little things like that kid that didn't look like us. They're letting us run around in that ball. I stop playing and tell it, 'I want to go for my ride now.' Then he lets me pretend I'm driving that big ball."

"How does he do that?" John wondered.

"He picks me up and lets me touch some controls," I explained.

"Is it like a steering wheel or a stick shift?" John asked.

"I don't see anything like that," I said. "There's something like a TV screen, and there are all these lines and colors and lights going across the screen."

"Are they pleasant to look at, or are they bothersome like static on a TV screen?" John asked.

"No. They're real clear and all different colors," I replied. "Fun to watch."

"And do you feel like you're going for a ride?" John asked.

"I think so."

"What's your brother doing?"

"I'm not sure. I'm not paying attention to him. I'm playing with the spaceship."

"So what's the next thing you remember?" John asked.

"They set me on a table so I can sit down. I'm going to lie down and take a nap."

"What did you remember when you woke up from your nap?"

"All those little things were standing around looking at me," I said.

"Did that make you kind of jump when you woke up?"

"No," I replied. "They were nice little things. My brother took a nap, too."

"And what happens when you all wake up?" John asked.

"My little friend told me that this was supposed to be a secret and he'd take me home now, but not to tell anybody. He said, 'This will be our little secret.' I told him, 'Okay.'"

"And is that what he does then?" John asked.

"We're back at the edge of the woods," I said.

"Is he with you?" John wondered.

"No."

"Do you know how you got to the edge of the woods?"

"No."

"All right," John said. "And there was a time around that age that you thought you saw angels. Where was it that you thought you saw angels?"

"In Gardendale, Alabama. I was outside. I had been riding my bicycle. I got off and laid it on the ground. I thought I saw something that looked like two angels."

"What made them look like angels?" John asked.

"They were floating in the air," I explained.

"What color were they?"

"Sort of white."

"White?" John asked.

"Sort of," I said again.

"Now you can take a good look at their faces," John requested. "Look and see if they have pretty blue eyes and blonde hair or whatever angels looked like to you then."

"Like the little thing that was in the woods," I said.

"Well, those didn't look like angels, did they?"

"No."

"But yet, now, that's what you see floating in the air?" John asked.

"No, it's not in the air now," I said. "It's in the woods."

"Two of them?" John asked.

"I just see one right now."

"Okay. Is this the same one that you played with?" John asked.

"Yeah," I replied.

"Okay. So you have known him a long time."

With the long-term relationship established, John soon brought me out of hypnosis.

The next evening John began my last session of that trip by having me again remember the night I was dropped off in the clearing and then taken to the conference room. He asked me to remember lying on the table after the creatures finished the vaginal scraping and ovary probe.

"What do you see now as you lie there?" John asked.

"A bright light shining in my eyes. The light causes me to not feel or see anything."

"See if you can hear anything," John requested.

"Little sounds," I said. "Between chirping and clicking."

"What do you think that's related to?" John asked.

"It's a method of communicating," I replied. "It has something to do with the Morse Code sound in my ear."

"So is the clicking sound in your head or just related to what you hear in your head?" John asked.

"It's related to what is in my ear. It doesn't make any sense."

"It doesn't have to make sense right now," John assured me. "Just describe what you're feeling and noticing."

"That's how they talk to me when they're not present," I said.

"Are you still in the bright light?"

"There's nothing shining in my eyes now. There's some kind of a silver spherical object above my abdomen."

"Notice what it does when you watch it for a while," John said.

"It's real fuzzy. I'm not sure."

"You must have asked them what they're doing," John mused.

"At that point I already knew what they were doing," I explained. "Trying to improve their race."

"Did you feel like they indicated that to you in some way?" John asked.

"No. They had already told me that at another time."

"Perhaps you can remember more about what they've already told you."

"They're using the eggs; they need them. At some time, I told them that if they needed them and if it would help them, then I would be glad to help them out."

"So you told them that you were willing to participate?" John questioned.

"Yes," I replied.

"So was this the only time they took eggs from you?"

"No."

"I wonder when the first time might have been."

"I don't remember."

"Do they tell you anything else about you or your participation?"

"I don't remember," I replied. I was still focusing on the activity aboard the craft. "Two creatures are doing something with the black box."

"Focus in on the black box and the two creatures. Watch very closely. What do you notice?"

"After the black box is brought over close to me, the needle goes into my ovary." I felt intense pain. "It hurts," I cringed.

"I know," John said sympathetically. "You don't have to feel the pain now. You can just focus on the black box."

"The two creatures open it," I went on. "The needle moves and puts something in the black box."

"What do they seem to put into the black box?"

"What was in the needle. They close it, and one creature walks away with it very carefully."

"How big is this box?" John asked.

"About the size of a transistor radio," I said.

"What's it made of?" John wanted to know.

"I haven't seen a substance like that."

"What does it remind you of?"

"The closest thing is metal, but it's not metal."

"Follow the action and see what happens next," John instructed.

"They put the black box in a compartment of the wall of the spaceship. I get up then. I don't leave right away. I stay in there and mess around with them for a while, but I don't remember anything else."

"Do you remember how you left?"

"No."

"Okay," John said. "Leaving this scene now, there was a time when you dreamed that something had some kind of relations with you. You can slowly sink back into feeling that dream and what you remember about the images in the dream. What do you notice as you think about that feeling?"

"I can't move, and I can't feel anything," I said.

"Is that what you're remembering?"

"Yeah."

"And as you remember not being able to move or feel anything, what do your eyes see?"

"It's a strange creature." I tried to describe it. "It's kind of brownish and looks reptilian. It's real thin. It has brownish eyes but with a gold glare. It's nasty looking."

"Are they the big black eyes with no pupil?" John asked.

"No. No. It's different. No. This eye has two colors. It's brown and gold and real glaring. I don't like to look at those eyes."

"Do they remind you of any type of animal?"

"Yeah. A reptile."

"What makes the eyes look reptilian?" John questioned.

"Glassy looking. Glaring."

"What does the rest of the head look like?"

"It's got ears, long pointed ears," I replied.

"Is the skin any particular color?"

"It's a light-colored brown."

"How does the mouth look?"

"It has pointed, uneven teeth. It's real ugly. I didn't want to look at it. I shut my eyes."

"Is there anything interesting or peculiar about the body?" John asked.

"It had scaly skin. It was the ugliest thing I've ever seen. It has ribs or something like that. The head reminds me of a gigantic snake's head. The hands have claws."

"Where are you?" John wondered.

"In my bed."

"What does the creature do?" John asked.

"That strange thing is raping me!" I exclaimed, feeling a sense of helplessness.

"Aren't you screaming or complaining?" John asked.

"I can't move, and I don't feel anything," I explained.

"Is there any type of communication?" John asked.

"No. I don't like that creature," I said emphatically.

"Is that the only creature around?"

"Yes."

"And this feels real to you?"

"Yes."

"It wasn't like an image on a screen or..."

"No."

"So even if it rapes you, you don't feel anything?"

"No, I don't," I told him again.

"What happens when this thing is done?" John asked.

"I don't remember."

"Did you pass out?"

"I don't remember."

"Okay," John said. "Well, let's move through time again. Let's move through time when you were in the clearing and the helicopter arrives. You're taken inside a conference room. You remember feeling dizzy, your head in your lap, but you can still hear. Notice all that you can as you will now remember everything. It may be hard to remember if you're drugged, but notice when you leave the chair."

"All I remember is being put on a stretcher," I said. "The guys are putting the stretcher in a truck of some kind."

"Notice any markings, numbers, designations," John instructed.

"I can't see anything," I explained. "I'm feeling too sick."

"Are you alone?"

"Other people get in there. I know they're driving me somewhere, but I don't remember anything else."

"Do you remember hearing any comments or remarks between the men as they sat there with you?" John asked.

"Yeah," I said.

"Who's talking?" John asked.

"I can't see him. I'm too sick to look at him," I explained.

"That's all right," John said. "You can hear them, though. What do they say?"

"He says, 'She knows too damn much. How are we going to handle this?'" The voice sounded like that of the man who talked to me in the conference room.

"And what do you hear?" John wanted to know.

"Somebody else...I don't recognize that voice...says, 'I don't know. This is a tough one.'"

"What seems so tough?" John wondered.

"I don't know," I replied, wondering the same thing.

"Do they give an indication as to what they know that you know?" John questioned.

"No," I replied.

"Do they ever talk about precautions?"

"I don't remember anything else," I answered.

"Do they talk about any kind of threat or harm?"

"Not after I get in the truck. They think I'm asleep. And I almost am."

"Is there anything else that you just happened to over-hear?" John wanted to know.

"No. I felt like I was about to pass out."

Since I could remember nothing further about that night, John brought me out of the hypnotic state. Since it was late, he and Grace left soon afterwards.

Before falling asleep, I went over and over the material we had explored thus far. I was annoyed that instead of answering questions for me, the hypnosis sessions were bringing up more questions. How could I have had meetings with aliens throughout my entire life and not remember them? Why could I never remember how I left the spacecraft? How, as children, could Seth and I have been taken away by the creature and my parents be unaware of it? Where was Mike when the reptilian creature raped me? Had I done something so bad that I deserved to be punished in that manner? Did that incident lead to the mysterious symptoms that landed me in the hospital in 1981? What else was said in the conference room, and why couldn't I remember it? And, most importantly, what did I know that was "too damn much"? I was upset that I would have to return home with these questions unanswered.

As I lay on the bed floundering in this sea of emotional turmoil, an image leaped into my mind. It was a room filled with fellow abductees and chalky-colored creatures with huge black eyes. As I puzzled over the meaning of this image and why I was even seeing such an image in my head, it was if a silent voice said to me, "God is with you, and the family of God is with you."

I interpreted this message as confirmation that the chalky-colored creatures who visited me were on God's side. I interpreted it as an indication that we abductees were in this unknown territory together. I interpreted it as assurance that by working together and loving each other, God's alien and abductee followers, with God's strength and leadership, could carry out our part in some magnificent, mysterious mission. Having been rescued from the waves of distress by this silent message, I was able to drift off to sleep, now feeling a sense of comfort and peace.

CHAPTER NINE

The next morning, May 22, 1991, I woke up unusually early and could not fall back asleep because of two disturbing dreams I had. In the first, I was violently jerked back and forth by a powerful vacuum-cleaner-like force. I glanced at the clock to see what time it was and noticed the electricity was off.

In the second dream, I was home when I received a phone call from a government agent named Maurice. He told me if I confessed, I would be forgiven. Then he said, apparently to someone who was with him, "Peggy, go get the tape recorder." Assuming that he planned to record my confession, I immediately hung up the phone. Soon afterwards, Maurice appeared at my door and demanded a confession. Laura and Kelly looked on in bewilderment as I told him I had done nothing wrong and had nothing to confess. I also told him the government already had copies of my documents and tapes and there was nothing new I could tell him. Then he said, "You were involved in the Gulf Breeze Incident." I insisted I had not been to the Gulf. Disappointed that he was unable to obtain a confession from me, he left.

These dreams disturbed me because I felt that, like others, they had elements of reality mixed in them. I wondered if the electricity really had gone off during the night and, if so, what had caused it. I especially was troubled by the phrase, "You were involved in the Gulf Breeze Incident" because I knew somewhere, sometime, a man had actually said that to me. But what did the incident involve? When did it occur? Why couldn't I remember? I had been to Gulf Shores twice on vacation. That is near Gulf Breeze. Could I have been abducted while there on vacation?

Grace met me for breakfast and we discussed these dreams, the results of my hypnosis sessions, and last night's silent message about the family of God. Then she drove me to the airport and saw me safely on the plane. Her concern was obvious and sincere; it was good to know I could count on her and others I had met in Springfield for further support or help if I needed it.

The first day back home, my throat was extremely sore and I could hardly talk. I had difficulty breathing and was so weak that I lay in bed all day. I could not understand how I had acquired this flu-like illness. To my knowledge, I had not been near anyone who was ill. And May was an odd time to come down with the flu, especially for a person who rarely gets sick. As I thought about my condition, I realized how easy it would be to eliminate someone merely by injecting germs or drugs.

Mike came home that night to discuss the results of my trip to Springfield. As I was changing clothes, he asked how I had gotten such a huge bruise on the back of my thigh. I had not noticed the bruise and had no knowledge of its origin. Examining it more closely, Mike said the bruise looked like a fresh one, and there was a red mark in the center that looked as if a needle had been inserted. The mark was a mystery; I knew I had done nothing to cause it.

Mike became angry when I told him about being kidnapped by men in green fatigues and taken to the conference room. He was angry the men violated my rights and the aliens abandoned me in the field. He felt if the aliens were my friends, they would not have done that.

It was good to know Mike believed my encounters were real and I was not crazy. Meeting other abductees on my second trip to Springfield, I had learned not all spouses are supportive. I felt very fortunate mine was.

I was sick for a week after returning from Springfield. I took the opportunity to lie around and digest the material uncovered through hypnosis. The conference room episode was the most upsetting. I had always been proud to be an American—to live in a place where I was free and to feel protected by our armed forces. Yet, the very people I thought were supposed to protect and defend me had treated me like a prisoner of war. The man wearing the blue uniform had called me a troublemaker. Why? What did he mean by that remark? I had done nothing to cause our military trouble. And what could I possibly know that was "too damn much"? I certainly didn't remember anything of importance.

I felt if the military was so concerned about what I knew, I was probably being monitored constantly. I felt I no longer had any privacy, as if all my dignity had been stripped away. I felt like a naked, hunted animal with no place to hide.

I also felt lonely. There was no one in Craston I felt comfortable talking with about the alien and military abductions. Not even Judith, since her husband was in the military. But the stress of being a victim of the alien phenomenon and the related government/military cover-up was tremendous. I could not keep it bottled up inside. I released some of my frustrations by regularly writing John Carpenter and by spending hours on the telephone talking with Seth, Lori, and fellow abductees I had met through John. The support of these individuals was invaluable in helping me cope.

After recovering from my illness, I searched through old photographs to see if I could find some of Seth and me the way we looked when we took the ride in *the big silver ball*. I found one that was identical, except for our clothing. Seth was only one year old in the photo; I was three. Since I had no memory of any kind prior to age three, the fact I remembered no alien encounters before then did not mean that none occurred. I wondered if the aliens had been visiting us since birth. Could it even be possible the aliens were responsible for our conception?

I had so many unanswered questions. I began to retire early at night to read my Bible, pray, and reflect on the meaning of my new discoveries of life. During these periods of quiet relaxation, I began to have occasional mental flashes. I suddenly remembered that "Ceto" was the name of the chalky-colored creature who had always comforted me and that his group told me the reptilian creature who raped me would never bother me again. I saw the side view of a cute little boy who looked about three years old as a silent voice told me, "That is your son."

In one flash I saw myself as an adult standing on a beach, all alone. A military vessel sat out in the ocean, seemingly shooting at something in the air. Then I heard someone call to me through a megaphone.

In another flash I saw a man wearing a gas mask, carrying a chalky-colored creature across his shoulder. The creature looked at me with fear in his eyes. Then I saw an airplane wobbling, as if it were about to crash.

Another flash showed a group of chalky-colored creatures coming down a ramp of a spaceship.

In another I saw a circle along with the message, "The circle is unbroken."

Another image revealed a spaceship which looked like two convergent saucers hovering in the air. Thin beams of light shining from its bottom formed a triangular configuration. The spaceship shot off, leaving pyramids where the light beams had been.

A separate picture involved dozens of missiles shooting across the sky from west to east, leaving billows of smoke in their paths. It was as if the planet were being destroyed, yet I was detached from the event, witnessing it from a distance.

There was a second mental flash seemingly painting a picture of our planet's destruction. Everything I saw in the background was brown: the sky, the plants, the water. I saw all types of animals dropping dead, one by one. I saw a father and mother and their two children on hands and knees, trying to crawl over the trunk of a dead, fallen tree to get to the water nearby. They seemed too near death ever to reach the water, but even if they did, its poisons would kill them. Again I witnessed the event from afar, this time with mixed emotions. I felt fortunate that I did not have to suffer this type of pain, yet I felt torn apart that I could do nothing to save this family or to alleviate their suffering.

Some of these mental flashes appeared to be messages from unknown sources; others appeared to be flashes of memory. Whatever they were, they were strange and unsettling. I did not know how to interpret them. I wondered how much more had been locked in the closets of my mind and when and where I could find the key to unlock them.

Not only was I plagued by these strange mental flashes, alien-related dreams intermingled with bits of reality continued to haunt me. On May 29, I dreamed something terrible was happening to me, something alien-related, and I was begging God to help me. As I cried out to God, I woke up, not remembering what had terrified me.

After going to bed on June 5, I saw flashes of blue light shine across my bedroom near the ceiling. They came from the direction of my window and moved toward the bathroom. I was home alone and too frightened to get out of bed and look out the window. Since our house has tall ceilings and my room is on the second floor, I was puzzled about the source of a light that could shine that high. I thought perhaps it was a helicopter, but I heard no accompanying sound.

Unable to stay awake for long, I fell asleep and dreamed I was sitting in the passenger side of my car. The fuel gauge indicated the gasoline tank was almost empty, and I worried about running out. But then I noticed the keys were not in the ignition, and although I saw no aliens, I concluded they must be causing the car to move. I looked up and noticed the sun roof was open. I assumed the aliens must have opened it since I hadn't.

Later I found myself lying on a low platform in unfamiliar surroundings. Three aliens were examining a man lying to my left. They put a cage-like piece of equipment on his nose. When they finished, they walked over and did the same to me. I felt a bit of pressure but no pain. Then they cut a little piece of skin from behind my ear. I was surprised it didn't hurt or bleed. These aliens were not members of Ceto's race. They appeared almost human, middle-aged with broad noses and prominent ears. They were naked, their long penises stiff against their abdomens. They spoke in English, with mono-tone voices. I asked them where they were from. They said there was no point in telling me because I had no concept of the location. I asked them why government agents were hassling me about my encounters with aliens. They burst out laughing. One of them explained it is because humans are so primitive and too wrapped up in governmental, politi-cal, and religious conflicts. I woke up, disappointed they didn't provide a more detailed explanation.

The night of June 23, I experienced another mental flash, this one especially disturbing. While I was reading my Bible, a silent voice told me I am needed to help spread the word about the existence and visitations of the aliens, through both speaking and writing. I was told the creatures will be visiting Earth more frequently and in greater numbers and humans need to be prepared.

"Oh, no," I silently argued. "Not me. No way! I can't get involved with this sort of thing. The military/government agents who have been monitoring me would make my life pure hell. It would bring suffering to my family. I can't do it."

But the mental flash continued. It told me the creatures would try to prevent anyone from doing any substantial harm to me, although I would be ridiculed and persecuted. "This is necessary," it added. "Someone must inform the public. We need your help with this."

I tried to ignore the message and told myself I must indeed be going crazy. I had always heard that "hearing voices" was a sign of insanity. Perhaps I needed to engage in normal activities more often so my sanity would be restored.

Two nights later I decided to call Judith but to avoid the subject of aliens. I had not heard from her since May 6 at which time she got upset that I again mentioned military cover-up activities, and I missed her companionship. Since I was tiptoeing around the subject of aliens, our conversation felt strained. Eventually the subject did come up. Judith reminded me our military had not investigated aliens since Project Blue Book. She told me she felt I had lied about current military cover-up activities, and since I lied about that, I must have lied about my alien encounters, too.

I was deeply hurt. I knew I had just lost someone I loved because of the alien phenomenon.

I went to bed depressed and, as usual, started reading my Bible before turning out the lights. As I read, I felt an inexplicable wave of peace flow over me and told myself, "I don't need Judith. I have God. I have my new friends in Missouri. I'll be okay."

Then one of those strange mental flashes attacked me again. "The episode with Judith was a test," it said. "This was a preview of the types of discrediting, ridicule, and emotional pain that will confront you as you tell others about your experiences. The fact that you dealt with the situation satisfactorily is proof that you can handle future situations of this nature. We need you to help spread the word so people will be prepared."

"I am definitely losing my mind," I thought.

I didn't understand the source of these mental flashes. Why did I not experience them before I started investigating alien encounters? What did they mean? Why were they occurring? I didn't understand them, and I didn't like them, especially the ones that told me to go out and make an ass of myself.

Dealing with the unexplained messages, flashes of memory, and strange dreams was emotionally draining enough, but other odd activities continued to invade my life as well.

On several occasions, our doorbell rang and wouldn't stop. Yet, when I went to the door, no one was there.

One afternoon, while driving to a management class I was taking, I hurried through a traffic light that was turning red. I was driving 50 mph. I noticed the dark blue vehicle behind me came through the light, too. I thought, "That driver is an idiot zooming through a red light like that. He must be in a big hurry."

I slowed down to 45 mph so he could get around me. Seeing that he didn't pass, I slowed down to 40 mph. He still didn't go around me. "Is he following me?" I wondered.

I slowed down to 35 mph, then to 20, and continued at that speed for quite a distance. He still failed to pass me, so I pulled off the road at a gas station. I noticed "U.S. Air Force" painted in yellow against the dark blue of the station wagon as it passed by. I pulled back onto the road, got into the left lane, and stopped next to the vehicle at a red light. There were three men inside, dressed in green fatigues. I looked them over carefully. One of them looked vaguely familiar, but I was not able to recall where I had seen him before. They looked away when they saw me staring at them and soon pulled off at an exit.

I was annoyed, confused, and frightened. It was obvious the men were following me, but why? Why were they playing these silly little games? Why didn't they come to my house, tell me they knew I was caught up in alien abductions, and discuss the situation like mature adults? I would have been happy to cooperate with them if they were honest with me.

My next disturbing incident occurred the night of July 1. A noise that sounded like footsteps on our oak stairs awakened me. Thinking Laura or Kelly must be up, I fell back asleep. The doorbell and Laura's voice awakened me again. Laura said the doorbell had been ringing for quite some time and she wondered why I hadn't checked it out. Groggy, I climbed out of bed, stumbled downstairs, opened the front door, and pushed the doorbell until it stopped ringing.

I went back to bed thinking perhaps the stuck doorbell was a sign the creatures were coming for a visit that night. I tried to stay awake because I wanted to remember the impending encounter consciously. But I could not hold my eyes open for long.

Then I dreamed my body was shaking and I knew it was caused by the force the creatures used to get me out of the house. In the dream I glanced at the digital clock to see the time. It was merely blinking. I reached over to my right to turn on the lamp so I could read the time on my mechanical clock. The lamp would not turn on; the electricity was off. I picked up the mechanical clock and turned it to see the time. It was 3:37 a.m. When I set the clock back on the table, I turned the face of it away from me because something was causing it to glare in my eyes. I was still shaking from the force. I felt slight pain in my left temple, more pronounced pain and swelling in the right side of my neck and head, and swelling in my eyes. Then I felt myself moving. My right eye quickly became so swollen I couldn't see out of it.

When I stopped moving, I saw white walls and knew I could not be in my own home. Then I saw a creature coming through a door. "Ceto!" I cried. But the creature did not respond; when it came nearer, I realized it was not Ceto.

We were soon in a different room. I could tell the creature was preparing to do something to my body. Frightened, I begged him, "Please don't hurt me." He smiled and chattered sounds that I knew meant, "No, no, I'm not going to hurt you." Then he picked up a piece of cream-colored tubing with a nickel-sized scope at the end which he attached to my body. I felt as if all the air were being removed from my body and then pressure, as if the air were being returned. I silently prayed, "God, please let me remember all of this."

When I woke up, the digital clock said 4:37. I wondered if I had been dreaming for the entire hour or if bits of my memories were real.

I went back to sleep for a while. When I finally got out of bed, I felt weak and nauseous. My arms and fingers were so swollen I could barely put on my watch and rings. As the day passed, my right arm became increasingly sore. I finally examined it and discovered three red marks that looked as if a needle had been inserted at those sites.

Then I remembered the dream I had on the night of May 22, my final night in Springfield. There were three similarities between that dream and this last one. In both, I was shaken by a force, the power went off, and I had unexplained marks on my body afterwards. I felt these similarities were not coincidental.

On the Fourth of July, I tried to get away from the alien phenomenon, to block it from my mind. Mike, our daughters, and I went to my parents' home for a holiday celebration where Seth, Lori, Lynda, and their children joined us. We played croquet, stuffed ourselves with homemade ice cream, and squirted each other with water guns in the back yard. Although I tried to have a good time, I silently resented celebrating liberty and freedom when I felt as if mine had been stripped away.

That evening, leaving Laura and Kelly with my parents, Mike and I drove to Tuscaloosa, Alabama, where Mike was currently working. We planned to spend the night in Mike's hotel room and fly to Chicago as soon as he got off work the next day in order to attend the annual international conference sponsored by the Mutual UFO Network (MUFON). It was to be our first UFO conference. Mike and I were eager to learn all we could about the phenomenon. Furthermore, John Carpenter felt that in order to protect myself, I should tell a few trustworthy people about my encounters with apparent military/government people.

When Mike and I arrived at his hotel, we noticed a vehicle with a U.S. government license plate parked near Mike's room. We thought it odd that a government employee would be spending the night in a hotel in Tuscaloosa, Alabama, on the Fourth of July, so we phoned Seth and gave him the license plate number as a precaution.

Mike got up early the next morning and left for work. I fell back asleep and had another strange dream. Several co-workers invited me to go out to lunch with them, but I decided to work through lunch instead. I was walking down a long corridor of the building when I heard someone whisper, "Leah." I looked around, but no one was there. I continued walking down the hall. A few seconds later, I again heard someone whisper my name. Looking in every direction, I still saw no one. I remembered I had heard that sometimes aliens call abductees by name. Then I felt a force engulfing me. I saw a door open and a very short creature walk toward me. He looked almost comical in his blue jumpsuit trimmed in red.

The scene changed; I found myself in what appeared to be a spaceship. But looking around, I knew it could not be an alien craft because the equipment was too primitive. I saw dials, gauges, and screens that all looked man-made. While I was examining this equipment, a door opened and in came the tiny creature I had seen earlier. A man followed him and stuck an L-shaped object into my left arm. He told me to leave it there, he would be back soon. He started to leave but stopped in the doorway as other men came into the room. They all looked like military types, with short hair and lean bodies. Two men wore black pants and white shirts with black stripes on the shoulders. One wore a khaki uniform. I did not notice the others' clothing.

The men surrounded me, and I demanded to know what they were doing with me. I told them I had a right to know. "If *you* were being followed by government agents, had your phones tapped, and were being harassed, you would want to know why," I explained.

One of the men said to another, "You know she's right. If you were in her shoes, you would want to know what's going on. I think you should tell her. She has a right to know."

As I searched their faces, hoping one of them would tell me, I noticed one had a fake moustache that had broken off, a piece of it stuck to his shirt. "By the way," I said, "Your moustache is falling off."

The others were looking at him and chuckling when I woke up.

"Damn!" I thought. "Why did I have to wake up before getting my questions answered?"

The dream was unsettling. Again I wondered if parts of it had actually happened and the memory was emerging in the form of a dream. John Carpenter had told me that could happen. I wondered if our military *was* working with aliens. The alien was the same one I dreamed about on July 1. Why did I dream about him twice in one week? And if this was simply a dream, where did the idea for this alien come from? I had never seen pictures or movies depicting an alien like that. He was the size of a toddler. He had hair matted on the back of his head, brushed sideways toward the center, which reminded me of a rubber baby doll I had as a child. He had a small slit for a mouth and rounded eyes.

I wondered if there truly was a man out there somewhere who wanted to tell me the truth about what was happening to me. Someone who cared about his fellow human beings and wanted to do what was right. I had to believe there was; I needed hope to cling to. Hope that someday I would learn the whole truth about the alien phenomenon and our government's interest in it.

At the MUFON conference, I was able to reveal my experiences involving military/government agents to several people John trusted. Now that others knew about my situation, eliminating me would not ensure the information I possessed would die with me. I felt a bit of comfort knowing that.

After we returned home from the conference, the puzzling mental flashes resumed. On July 13, I saw an image of gigantic rocks with objects carved in them: a four-pointed star, a round object resembling an ancient coin, and the side of an unidentifiable animal. Then I saw concentric circles, spiraling circles that were open at the beginning and end, an airplane propeller, and a wagon wheel; these were all spinning counterclockwise. I felt these objects were somehow connected to the crop circles that had been appearing throughout the world. The last image I saw was a tractor plowing up a field. Caskets containing chalky-colored creatures were buried there.

More images occurred the next night. First, the spinning circles and spirals appeared. When they vanished, I saw men dressed in green fatigues climb into an opening in the side of a knoll. Camouflaged doors hid the entrance when they were shut. Men outside the facility climbed into a jeep. One of them took out a pair of binoculars and looked up into the bright, blue sky. That scene changed, and I saw different kinds of angels, then the rotating circles again.

Soon after seeing these images, I fell asleep and received a message as I dreamed. Or perhaps I received it while I was awake momentarily; I'm not sure. The gist of the message was that human thought processes are too limited, that we humans put unnecessary constraints on those processes and we ought to unleash them.

The mental flashes were occurring so frequently I began to believe they were significant somehow, that there was a purpose behind them. One I did not understand, but one I was not to ignore. But where did these messages come from? Were they from God? Were they from the creatures? Were they creations of my own mind? Were they from a faction of our government or military conducting sadistic mind control experiments on me? Were they experiences blocked from my conscious memory that were now leaking out?

I told Mike I could no longer pursue my doctorate as I had originally intended. At the MUFON conference, I had met other people experiencing similar puzzling mental flashes and dreams of alien intrusions, and learned it was unlikely they would cease. Dealing with them had begun to require so much of my time and energy that a life dedicated to concentrated study was now out of the question. It was ironic; one of the reasons we had moved to Craston was so I could get my doctorate. In a way, I felt like a failure; in another, I felt as if something more important lay in store for me, but I did not yet know what it was.

CHAPTER TEN

I went back to Springfield for another set of hypnosis sessions the last week of July, 1991. I made the long drive alone, using the time to think about all that had happened since the previous July when the conversation at my parents' kitchen table sparked my inquiry into possible UFO encounters.

Much had happened since then. Hypnosis had revealed my alien encounters were real and not merely dreams. I had begun to have strange mental flashes I did not understand. And I had learned whatever was happening to me seemed to be of great interest to certain government and military personnel. Yet, I felt no closer to getting the answers I so desperately needed. Again I hoped the next set of hypnosis sessions would answer these questions.

I had previously mentioned to John that I remembered having twenty minutes of missing time in December, 1990, so John decided to explore this incident in our first session. Before starting the relaxation process, John asked me to describe for him and Grace what I remembered consciously about that December evening.

I told them I had driven Kelly and her best friend to the movies on the far side of town. It should have taken twenty-five minutes to drive back home, yet I arrived home forty-five minutes later, feeling dazed and perplexed about the loss of time. Soon I had to drive back to the movies to pick up the girls. Focusing on nearby security lights as I drove down a road near our home, I experienced a frightening flashback of a light shining in my rear-view mirror. The next morning, for no apparent reason, I awoke with lower back pain, which for several days was so severe I could barely sit or stand.

Since I consciously could recall no further details related to this incident, John began hypnosis.

Then I remembered the temperature was warm for December. A slow rain fell softly on my windshield as I drove the girls to the movie. As they got out of the car, Kelly told me to pick them up at 9:30. I began the drive back home. As I approached our neighborhood, I noticed a bright white light shining in my car. I was unable to determine its source. Soon I saw red reflecting in my rear-view mirror and realized it was the result of light reflecting off the stop sign behind me. Although I could not remember pulling off the road and stopping the car, I found myself standing outside, wondering when it had quit raining and noticing an eerie quietness. I no longer saw the bright light. Instead I saw an object shoot through the sky and vanish, and a helicopter circling the area. I drove home, looked at the kitchen clock, and with no memory of the strange encounter, wondered why it had taken me so long to get home from the movies.

Since I was unable to remember anything else about that night, John brought me out of hypnosis. I was disappointed with the session because there seemed to be gaps of time still missing. What I remembered would hardly fill twenty minutes.

While thinking about this incident later, I remembered that after I pulled off the road, a chalky-colored creature appeared next to my car, opened my door, took my hand, and helped me out. But I could remember nothing further.

The next evening's hypnosis session was more productive. John first decided to investigate the night of July 1, when my doorbell stuck. After getting me into the relaxed state, he asked me to concentrate on being in bed and what first caused me to stir.

"It sounds as if somebody's walking on the stairs," I said. "I think Laura or Kelly must be up."

"Okay," John said. "Notice now if you just go back to sleep or if you continue to be aware of whether somebody's in the house. Maybe it's just your daughters up and around, and that's all there is to it. See what you remember now as you relive that moment." John paused for a few seconds. "What do you notice? You're feeling something. What do you notice?"

"Somebody's in my room," I replied. "Somebody's saying, 'Hold still. Be still. Hold still, damn it.'"

"Does the voice seem real?"

"I'm not sure," I said, feeling groggy. "I just want to go to sleep."

"Move ahead another moment in time," John instructed. "What's the very next thing you're aware of?"

"The doorbell's ringing. It's stuck. It won't stop. Laura comes into my room and says it has been ringing for a long time. She asks why I haven't gotten up to turn it off. I go downstairs. I'm real sleepy; I almost fall down. I start to open the door but Laura says, 'Wait a minute.' She asks me if I turned off the security system, and I tell her that I didn't. So Laura goes to my telephone and cuts it off. I open the door and push the doorbell until it stops ringing. Then I lock the door and go back upstairs. I ask Laura if she was up a little while ago, and she says she wasn't. I sit down on the bed and turn the security alarm back on with the phone."

"What were your thoughts about the doorbell?" John asked.

"I think the creatures are probably messing with it. I'm real sleepy, but I want to stay awake in case the creatures do come. But they don't come, so I go back to sleep."

"Move ahead in time," John instructed, "and notice anything now that disturbs your sleep or whether you sleep peacefully until morning."

"I'm sick. My stomach hurts," I said.

"What do you do for your stomach?" John asked.

"I can't do anything," I explained. "I'm too sick. I feel severe pain in the center of my stomach. My head is swelling. I'm dizzy, weak and shaking."

"You feel nauseous, but you can't move?" John asked.

"No, I'm too weak," I explained. "I feel too bad. I'm lying on my stomach, holding it. I want to die. I just want to die."

"Move forward in time now," John said, "and see what you do about this or what happens next."

"I'm lying on my back with the chalky-colored creatures around me. They're looking at me. I don't understand what happened. I feel okay now. My stomach doesn't hurt. I'm okay."

"Are you still in your bedroom?"

"No," I answered. "The light's too bright. The creatures are just looking at me. I wonder why they're just standing around me looking. They don't do what they usually do to me. One of them touches my forehead. One of them opens my eyelid and looks in my eye. One of them says, 'We told you we'd take care of you. You're going to be okay.' He says it with his eyes. They always talk with their eyes."

"Move ahead a little bit," John said. "What's the next thing you notice happening?"

"They help me sit up. My right eye feels a little swollen. And the right side of my head. I want to go home and go to bed."

"What do you notice after you sit up?" John asked.

"One of them takes his hand and rubs it across my face. He's checking me out, like someone would touch a person to see if he has a fever. They hold me up for a minute or two. Then they let go. I want to go home."

"What's the next thing that takes place?" John wondered.

"I'm back in bed," I answered.

"Now, you had a dream in which you saw humans and what looked like human-made machinery. Switch to that for a moment. Contemplate that dream and see if anything more comes to you about that."

"I just keep seeing those men," I said. "A group of men."

"What about this group of men?" John asked.

"It's not clear. I don't know where I am," I explained.

"You don't know when, or where you are. I turn you loose to explore anything you want to look at. Think for a moment, and then tell us what you are curious about that you want to take a closer look at."

"It's so confusing. I don't know who those men are. I don't know where I am," I said, upset that I still could not get my bearings.

"Do they feel real, or do they feel like a dream again?" John wanted to know.

"No, they're real," I said emphatically, "but I don't know where I am. I don't know who they are. They call me by my first name. I don't know why they do that."

"These men look like normal men?" John asked.

"Yes."

"How are they dressed?"

"One of them has on a white shirt, the one with dark brown hair and a moustache. They all have short hair. One man has on a khaki-colored uniform."

"Who's in charge?" John wanted to know.

"I think the one in the khaki uniform," I replied. "He told the guy with the white shirt to give me some kind of medicine."

My memory was cloudy; I could remember nothing else other than the man in khaki saying something about giving me a certain number of cc's.

John brought me out of hypnosis at that point. I complained about not being able to remember much about the latter incident. John and Grace explained that if I had been given a shot, it would probably be difficult for me to recall additional details.

Back in my hotel room, unable to sleep, I went over and over the session we had just completed. All sorts of questions raced through my mind as I reviewed the sequence of events in the first incident we explored. Why did my dream include a creature different from those I remembered under hypnosis? Whose footsteps did I hear on the stairs? Who was the man who told me to hold still? Was he alone? Who or what was responsible for the three injection marks I discovered on my arm the next day? If the man was responsible, was he trying to kill me? If so, why? Was someone trying to prevent me from attending the MUFON conference in Chicago? How ill would I have become if the creatures had not visited me that night? Could I have imagined the presence of the human? Could I have imagined the entire incident? No. At least I knew the answer to my last question. I had three marks on my arm to prove that *something* occurred.

I was equally frustrated over my inability to remember the remainder of the second incident. John and Grace's explanation of possible drug interference did little to console me. Who were these men who had given me a shot? Why did they do it? When did it happen? Where was I? What type of drug was I given? Would it have any long-term effects? Why did I not remember this event consciously? I wondered how many more such incidents were blocked from my memory and if they would ever surface into my consciousness.

CHAPTER ELEVEN

The next evening John decided to explore some of the mental flashes that had been disturbing me. After the relaxation process, he asked me to describe what I remembered about a ship firing at something in the air.

"It doesn't make any sense," was my first comment.

"All right. What do you see that doesn't make any sense?" John asked. "You know not to hold anything back. Tell it all."

John had learned from experience that if I didn't want to face what I remembered in the hypnotic state or if I didn't understand what I was experiencing, I hesitated to verbalize it.

"I'm going out in the ocean to the ship," I said reluctantly. "It doesn't make any sense. I'm in a little boat."

"Look in this boat and see if you're alone."

"I'm facing one man. A young guy. He's wearing a white uniform. This...this can't happen!"

John ignored my protest. "Does he acknowledge your presence in any way?"

"I'm kind of dazed," I explained. "I don't know what's going on."

"Had you been watching something before this?" John asked.

"I don't know. I don't know what I'm doing out there. The boat starts out from the sand and goes out toward the ship on the ocean. There's a rope ladder coming off the ship. I have to climb up it. I don't think I can be there! I don't think this can happen!"

"Well, stay with what's going on," John requested. "Go ahead and follow the action. Feel the rope ladder with your hands and feet. Describe all that you're seeing."

"I don't have any shoes on," I noticed. "The rope's rough. It's high up. It takes me a long time to get to the top."

"Do you hear anything?" John asked. "Listen."

"A helicopter," I replied. "I hear a helicopter somewhere."

"What is it doing? Flying in a straight line from one place to the other?"

"I'm not paying attention to it," I explained. "I'm looking at the rope."

"So climb up the ladder now and see if there's anyone behind you."

"I'm not looking behind me," I said.

"Keep climbing. What happens now?" John asked.

"When I get to the top of the rope, a guy in a Marine Corps uniform helps me into the ship. I think, 'Why is he wearing a dress uniform on a ship?'"

"Does he seem glad to see you, or what kind of reaction do you notice as you arrive?"

"There is no reaction from that man. He helps me onto the ship, and that's it."

"Move ahead just one little bit," John instructed, "and see what takes place now."

"I don't see anything. I'm getting real dizzy."

"Did someone touch you?"

"I don't remember."

"Fight the dizziness and see all that you can see," John requested.

"I can't see anything. I'm going to pass out," I explained.

"Do you see anything before you pass out? Notice what all you've seen since you came aboard, and notice if there was anything unusual or whether everything seemed probably like what you'd see on a ship."

"No!" I resisted. "This can't happen! No!"

"Tell me what you see now," John ordered.

"They've got one of those creatures! His eyes! His eyes! I see his eyes!"

"Okay," John said. "Freeze the picture right now! Freeze it!"

"They're going to kill him!" I said, feeling tears come to my eyes. "He's lying on the deck of the ship. He wants me to help him, but I can't...they're holding me. They're holding me back. They won't let me help him!"

"Where did they get him?" John asked.

"I don't know," I said. "He's afraid!"

"And you really feel that," John said sympathetically.

"You really feel it for him. How can you see that he's scared?"

"His eyes," I explained. "They always talk to me with their eyes."

"Now let the action unfreeze," John directed, "and move ahead slightly in time and see what takes place now."

"I'm dizzy. They take me somewhere else. They're sort of dragging me. I don't want to go with them. I want to help the creature."

"The creature's still lying there?" John asked.

"Yeah."

"All right," John said. "So they take you somewhere. Follow that and see where they take you."

"Down some stairs," I explained. "Metal stairs. The first ones are warm; the ones at the bottom are not. I'm getting dizzy again. The moving makes me feel yukky. I feel dizzy and weak. I don't know where they're taking me."

"What reason would they have for wanting you there?"

"I don't know," I answered.

"How real does this seem right now?" John wanted to know.

"Too real," I replied. "Too real. I don't want it to be. I don't want it to happen!"

"Go on and see where you end up," John requested.

"I can't go anywhere else," I explained. "I'm too sick. I have to sit down."

"So if you're sitting down, what does the room look like?" John asked.

"I can't see it," I replied. "I'm too sick. I put my head in my lap. My head's too heavy."

"So what do you hear?"

"I ask them what they're going to do with the creature, and they say, 'Don't worry; we'll take care of him.' I want to go help him!"

"So what happens now?" John asked.

"Somebody comes and stands in front of me, but I can't look at him because I feel too sick. I just sit there. My head feels heavy. I feel weak and dizzy."

"You had another memory flash or image come to you of some man carrying a creature over his shoulder," John said. "Does that fit into here anywhere, or is that something entirely different?"

"He's on the beach," I replied.

"Who's on the beach?" John asked.

"The man carrying the creature," I told him.

"And where are you?"

"Standing on the beach."

"What had you been doing, and where did the man come from?"

"I don't know. I don't know."

"Back up and see if you can remember the first glimpse you had of either the man or the little creature."

"I think we were on that spaceship," I said.

"Where's the spaceship?" John asked.

"On the sand."

"What does it look like?" John wanted to know.

"This doesn't make sense," I replied.

"Well, just describe what you see," John requested. "Just state the facts. What do you see?"

"It's on the ground. It's a bit dome-shaped, tilted sideways on the ground. I don't understand what happened."

"How close is it to the water?" John asked.

"It's real close," I responded. "It's right on the beach. I don't know where I am. There aren't any buildings there. I don't know where I am!"

"So you feel that you and the creature may have been aboard the craft at some point. What were you doing on the spaceship?" John asked.

"There are more creatures on the spaceship," I said. "They just do the same things they always do."

"Same old stuff. Do they show you anything new? Was there anything different about this particular visit?"

"It can't happen!" I resisted again.

"What can't happen?" John prodded. "Tell us what it is that can't happen. You can't make those decisions by yourself."

"The spaceship's in the air, not very high up. I can see out of an opening, sort of like a window, but not exactly. I can see the ocean and that ship."

At that point, I remembered feeling a jolt. "I don't think this can happen!" I said. "It feels as if we're falling!"

"Why would you start to fall?" John questioned.

"I don't know," I replied.

"What are the creatures doing at this point?" John asked.

"I don't know," I answered. "We're going too fast. I don't know where they are. I don't know what they're doing. We're going too fast."

"You're feeling something very intensely right now," John noticed. "What do you feel?"

"My head. It hurts. I hit something."

"So you hit your head. Did you just bump it slightly, or did you really bang it good?"

"It hurts real bad," I replied.

"Did you pass out?"

"I'm not sure."

"How do you get out of the craft?"

"There's a big opening. I just walk out onto the sand."

"Does it all seem like a dream?" John wanted to know.

"No."

"Are you all alone?"

"That man's carrying the little creature. He's alive."

"How can you tell?" John asked.

"I can tell by the eyes," I explained. "He moves his head and looks at me. The man walks toward the ocean with him." I paused. "Somebody's yelling at me."

"What are they yelling?" John asked.

"'Stay right there! Don't move!' I don't know who says it."

"Somebody else is there?" John asked.

"Somebody yells," I replied. "I don't know what's going on. My head hurts. I don't know if the sound is coming from the helicopter or the boat."

"Is it a natural-sounding voice, or does it sound amplified?" John wanted to know.

"It sounds amplified," I told him, "but I'm not sure. My head hurts. It feels as if it's going to explode."

"What happens next?" John questioned.

"The helicopter is coming close to the creature," I answered. "I think they put the creature in the helicopter, but I'm not sure; I'm looking at that life boat."

"How did it get there?"

"I don't know. Two men tell me to come get in the boat. They have to help me because I'm real dizzy."

"How does your head feel?" John asked.

"It hurts real bad."

"What part of your head's hurting?"

"Just the back."

"So they have to help you into the boat. Are you going willingly? Did you resist?"

"No. I feel too bad to fight with them. My head hurts; I feel dizzy."

"All right," John said. "We know what happens on board the deck. You're taken down the metal stairs, feeling very sick and not being able to hold your head up. What happens to the rest?"

"I don't remember," I replied.

"One last big question," John said slowly. "How did you get home?"

"I don't remember. The last thing I remember is sitting on the step with my head in my lap," I explained.

"Does it seem like a dream?" John wanted to know.

"No," I said reluctantly.

I went back to my hotel room that night more upset and confused than ever and spent most of the night trying to make sense of everything. I could not understand how an individual could be involved in an event that important and then completely forget about it. If it did happen, when? I tried to remember times in my life when I had physical symptoms that might be related to a head injury. On several occasions I had severe headaches. And there was a period of time in which I became dizzy in the grocery store or whenever I stood up for long. I also remembered my dentist's concern over my teeth being loose for no apparent reason. But those problems eventually went away by themselves, and I forgot about them. Therefore, I could not pinpoint an exact date. I had always tried to go on with my daily activities even when I felt bad, so I *could* understand how I could be in a crash and not pay too much attention to a resulting headache.

But I could *not* understand how I could have gotten back home from the beach without anyone even noticing my absence. Travelling from the beach to almost every place I had ever lived would have required at least a couple of hours' time, even by air. However, my family had gone to the beach several times for a vacation. Could I have been abducted one of those times?

There was another puzzling question. If the incident did

occur, why didn't the military eliminate me on the spot? Was it because they gave me drugs that were meant to erase my memory of the incident permanently?

If so, that could explain why I was followed, why I was watched in restaurants, why I heard odd noises on my telephones, and why so many other unexplained things began to happen when I started investigating my possible alien encounters. Perhaps the government was worried about just how much I would remember and what I would do with the information. Perhaps my knowledge of this incident was what the military officer meant when he said I knew *too damn much*.

If the incident did not occur, then what was wrong with me? Why would my mind remember something that did not happen? I had never seen a television program or read a book about an incident of that sort. So if the incident did not occur, how did the memory originate? Was it a result of mental illness?

No. No. For the past year, there had been too much evidence of military/government interest in me; they would not spend that much time and money monitoring a woman merely because they were interested in her insanity. Their interest in a woman remembering a military secret would make more sense.

Another thought occurred to me. Now that I had remembered this incident, what would happen? Would I be killed? I told myself that probably I would have been eliminated already if someone wanted me dead. But I didn't know that for certain, and I became filled with fear. And I knew there was nothing anyone could do to help me.

CHAPTER TWELVE

For the final session of my third trip to Springfield, John decided to explore my recollections of blue flashes of light in my bedroom and my subsequent dream of June 5. After John got me into the relaxed state, he asked me to describe what I had seen before falling asleep that night.

I described the blue flashes as gaseous-looking blobs approximately a foot long. Five of them floated in succession from my bedroom window toward my bathroom. I thought perhaps someone was shining a light into the room that was reflecting off the ceiling fan, perhaps a helicopter was shining its lights into the room, or perhaps aliens were sending something into the room. I did not get up to investigate the light because I was too frightened and too tired. I soon fell asleep.

"So proceed into your night," John directed. "Describe what you experience now as you relive that dream."

"I feel as if I'm being moved in a dark tunnel," I said.

"Well, go on," John prodded. "How else does the dream proceed?"

"No, that's not a dream," I insisted.

"As you feel yourself being pulled through a dark tunnel, what's the next thing you remember?"

"I'm outside looking at the sky, but I don't know if it's before or after going through the tunnel," I replied.

"You're not sure of the time frame," John said. "All right. So you're outside where?"

"In the front yard, looking at the stars," I answered. "I'm watching red lights move through the sky from west to east."

"Are they in a particular formation or pattern?"

"Similar to a barrel that is wider in the center."

"How big is this object?"

"I can't tell. It's too far away. I think it's a spaceship, but I haven't seen a spaceship like that before. The lights are coming toward me."

"What are you noticing now?" John asked.

"I can't see anything. There's red light around me. I can't see anything else. It's a warm light, real bright."

"Is it the first light that you saw?" John wondered.

"No."

"Do you hear anything?"

"No."

"Do you feel anything physically besides warmth?"

"I just feel warm, calm, peaceful. Sedated. It's making me feel groggy."

"What happens next? Where are you?"

"I don't know what this thing is!" I said. "I'm lying in some kind of a container. It's sort of like glass, sort of like plastic. It's clear, but I don't know what it is. I'm tingling all through my body. It starts in my head. It's like pulses, charges of some kind. My hands and feet are tingling. I want it to stop!" I winced, pain from the shock treatment becoming unbearable.

"Well, move on through that," John said. "Move ahead in time a little bit more."

"It's dark in here," I went on. "There's a red glare coming from somewhere. The glass is not over me anymore. I can't move. I can't look around."

"Is it because of the tingling feeling, the electrical charge or whatever that went through you?" John asked.

"I'm not sure why."

"You didn't notice when the glass case left?" John wanted to know.

"No."

"What else do you notice?" John asked.

"I can't see anything," I replied. "Everything's black."

"Is that because the lights are off?"

"I think...I think I must have blacked out for a minute." I paused. "My right ear hurts."

"What kind of sensation?" John wondered.

"Constant pain behind my right ear," I said. "It's...it's gone now. It just hurts a little bit. I feel as if somebody's here, but I don't see them. It's real dark."

"Okay," John said. "So move ahead a little step in time and see how the scene changes."

"I feel like I've been sedated or something," I replied. "I

can barely see forms. There's some kind of black machine over my head. I think they're going to take X-rays with it."

"Who are *they*?" John asked.

"They're people!" I remarked. "I keep expecting to see the creatures, but they're people. Humans. That man is wearing a white lab coat."

"What are *you* wearing?" John wondered.

"I'm not sure," I answered. "There's a sheet over me."

"Do you feel as if you're on board a spacecraft?" John asked.

"It looks like a hospital room. I'm on a hospital bed, like an operating table. There's another operating table to my left and a bluish-green curtain, but it's open. There's medical equipment in here."

"Do you hear the voices of doctors and nurses?"

"I see only men, but I can't see them clearly because I've been sedated or something. I don't know where I am. I don't know how I got here. I don't know who these people are. They're standing against the wall."

"How many of them?" John wanted to know.

"Three. One of them is wearing a white lab coat. I can't see his pants; I'm lying down. I think the man in the khaki uniform is the man who told me I hadn't seen a spaceship."

"Oh, in the conference room!" John remarked. "This man is there?"

"I'm not sure; I think it's the same man," I said.

"Well, you're not sure because you were not feeling good either time," John explained. "You feel drugged now and you felt drugged then."

"My ear is hurting again," I told John.

"Your right ear?" he asked.

"Yes. It hurts badly!"

"Well, move on through that pain," John instructed. "What happens next?"

"The man in the khaki uniform asks the guy in the lab coat, 'Did you get it okay?' The man in the lab coat says, 'No problem.' Then the man in khaki says, 'I think it's time to give her another shot.' The man in the lab coat says, 'Yeah, I've got it right here.' He reaches over to the other table and picks it up."

"Do you see what he picks up?" John wanted to know.

"Yeah. It's a syringe, a needle," I explained. "They've got my arms strapped down! I can't move! I don't want him to give me the shot, but I can't move."

"Do you feel the shot?" John asked.

"Yeah. It's going in my left arm. It stings. I call them dirty names; I'm mad. I say, 'I wish you'd leave me alone. What do you want, you dirty bastards? Leave me alone!'"

"What do they do when you say that?" John questioned.

"They tell me to shut up, that I've caused them enough trouble already," I replied.

"All right," John said. "Do you remember anything else about that episode?"

"I'm getting dizzy again," I explained. "I feel like I'm going to pass out."

"Is the black machine still over your head?" John asked.

"I can't see it," I replied. "I've got my eyes shut. I think I'm going to pass out."

I could remember nothing else about the incident, so John brought me out of hypnosis.

Alone in my hotel room later that night, I reviewed everything we had explored under hypnosis thus far. With each session, the web was becoming more complex. Back in March, I had expected, at most, to discover that if my alien-related dreams turned out to be real events, I had experienced only a few encounters with aliens. I had thought a few hypnosis sessions would uncover all of my experiences, that I could deal with them and stuff them away into a corner of my mind, and get back to a normal life. But that was not the case. Instead I discovered alien encounters had occurred throughout my entire life and were still occurring. And some of the encounters involved not aliens, but humans.

Tonight's session shocked me because I had expected to uncover an alien abduction after remembering the blobs of light floating through my bedroom. But instead I found myself in what appeared to be a hospital room staffed by humans. How did I get to the hospital? Where was it? I felt it must have been a military facility since one of my captors was in uniform. Did the incident occur the night of June 5 after I saw the strange blue flashes in my room, or was it a different time? What I remembered under hypnosis certainly differed from my dream of June 5. And what caused my ear to hurt?

Did the men remove an implant previously put there by aliens? I no longer heard beeps in my right ear. Could that explain why? What was the purpose of the transparent container? Why did my captors subject me to shock treatment? Why did machinery scan my body? What additional medical procedures were performed on me? Would they have adverse long-term effects? How did I get back home? Why could I remember none of the incident before now?

Questions, questions, and more questions. Why in the hell couldn't I get answers? Damn it, I wanted answers!

But again I would have to return to Craston with my questions unanswered.

CHAPTER THIRTEEN

I remained in Springfield for an extra day to attend a meeting of the abductee support group John had organized. Talking with people who had experienced similar encounters was therapeutic. I felt a bond with them. However, since none of them had ever remembered being abducted by humans, I was left alone in dealing with those memories.

I planned to leave for home after eating breakfast with Grace on July 31, but John persuaded me to remain in Springfield one more day. He wanted to make me copies of the cassette tapes of the hypnosis session involving the beach incident to take home; he would not have an opportunity to make the copies until he got off work that evening.

John brought the tapes to my hotel on his way to work the next morning. Soon afterwards, I started my drive back to Craston.

For the first two hours I listened to tapes that one of the support group members had given me. Although the tapes were encouraging, what made me feel even better was knowing my fellow abductee cared about me, understood what I was going through, and was reaching out her hand. I hoped the love, understanding, and care we all felt for each other would get us through the confusion and uncertainty we faced.

I turned off the cassette player and, for the next hour, drove through gently rolling hills, soaking in their beauty. As I passed quaint little shops in a small town in Arkansas, I promised myself to stop and browse on one of my future trips. I drove slowly through the outskirts of town, contemplating the sense of peace portrayed there.

Suddenly I heard the screech of tires and thought, "Oh, my God, someone's about to have an accident!" Then I heard a crash.

When the frightening noise ended, I could see nothing but darkness. I heard voices saying, "Ma'am, are you all right? Ma'am? Ma'am? Are you all right?" I felt severe pain in my head and neck, realizing that *I* was involved in the crash I had heard. Dark vapors began to form in front of me. Slowly they became lighter-colored, blurred images. Finally my vision returned.

I cringed in fear when I saw a man in uniform standing next to my door, telling other people to stand back.

"Who are you?" I demanded as I tried to look at him.

"Don't move!" he said. "I'm a county deputy. Where are you hurt?"

"Just my head and neck," I said as I tried to look at him again, catching a glimpse of his badge.

"Don't move your head! Sit still!"

"What happened? Where am I?"

The deputy told me I had just passed through town. "Apparently, a car was turning left in front of you," he explained, "and a van hit you from behind."

I tried to look in my rear-view mirror. With pain shooting through my head and neck, I was able to catch only a glimpse of a big, white van with a crushed front.

"This is not my jurisdiction," the deputy explained. "I need to call the city marshal. Don't move. I'll be right back and stay with you until he arrives."

Soon the marshal arrived, introduced himself, and announced that an ambulance was on its way.

"No! I don't want to go to the hospital!" I screamed as memories of my final hypnosis session flooded back.

"We can't force you to go to the hospital, but you took a pretty bad lick. I think it would be a good idea to get checked out."

I became almost hysterical and explained to the marshal that I possessed some sensitive information that put me in jeopardy and I was afraid to be alone in a strange town. Then I realized how foolish I must sound to a complete stranger; the marshal probably thought the accident was causing me to become delirious. But he seemed to believe what I told him.

"Ma'am," he said, "I'm in charge of this town and I promise that you'll be safe here."

He told me he could station armed guards at the door of my hospital room if I needed to be admitted. He promised to have my car taken away and locked inside a building. And he promised to check on me at the hospital as soon as he took care of all the other details concerning the accident.

The man reminded me of Marshal Matt Dillon, and I believed he would do whatever he could to ensure my safety. Knowing the dangers of receiving a blow to the head, I agreed to be transported to the hospital for X-rays.

It seemed an eternity before the ambulance arrived. The technicians put a brace on my neck before helping me from the car and then strapped me onto a stretcher. I relived the horrors of being strapped down and given shots by apparent military men. The horror continued at the hospital as a black X-ray machine scanned the upper portion of my body. I wanted to jump off the table and run far away from the X-rays and straps and people in white lab coats. It took all the composure I could muster to remain still until my examination was complete.

The examination revealed there was no damage to my head or neck, so I was released with a prescription for pain-killers and advice that I remain in town overnight in case unforeseen complications arose.

The marshal picked me up from the hospital and drove me to the garage where my car was stored. Only the trunk and rear end were damaged, so I was able to drive it. I followed the marshal to headquarters so I could sign papers pertaining to the accident. I asked him about the person who hit me. He showed me the driver's license of a man whose residence was in a nearby town. The accident report showed the driver was following too closely and skidded seventy-six feet before hitting me. The driver was uninjured, but the accident appeared to be legitimate.

With the advice of the hospital staff and feeling too shaky to drive farther anyway, I checked into a hotel for the night. I failed to get my prescription filled because I wanted to remain as alert as possible in case military/government agents lurked nearby. The next morning I awoke with only a slight headache and discomfort in my chest. The experience proved to me that a person can have a severe headache, dizziness, and disorientation from a crash and feel only slight discomfort soon afterwards, that the spaceship crash at the beach could indeed have occurred without my being seriously injured. The thought flashed through my mind that perhaps the aliens staged my automobile accident to teach me this, but I quickly brushed aside the thought because I believed that the aliens would be more inclined to protect me rather than hurt me.

I arrived in Craston safely and, despite delayed swelling in my chest from the accident, resumed my routine, only to be faced with an autumn filled with perplexing events.

On August 12, I left Laura's car at a repair shop to have the air conditioner repaired. Later that day a mechanic phoned me to say the tires needed to be rotated, too, and he would need to keep the car overnight because a part he ordered for the air conditioner would not be in until the next day. I gave him permission to do that.

The next day as Laura was driving home from the repair shop, the front right tire fell off. Her car skidded all over the road at a busy intersection. Miraculously, she avoided hitting another vehicle and was not seriously injured, although the front end of the car was badly damaged. Apparently, someone at the repair shop had forgotten to tighten the nuts on the wheel.

On August 30, as Laura was driving Kelly to a football game, she was involved in another accident. She slowed to make a left turn, the car immediately behind her stopped, and a third car rammed the one behind Laura, pushing it into her. Again, no one was seriously injured.

Dealing with vehicle repairs took all my free time in August and the first half of September. In addition to the three accidents, there were three breakdowns. Laura's air conditioner had malfunctioned in early August. Her water pump broke on September 3. My air conditioner malfunctioned on September 7, after leaving it outside during the night at my parents' house; I always kept it locked in the garage at home.

I was puzzled at these problems because I kept our cars in good condition, taking them to the shop for routine maintenance as the owners' manuals suggested. Furthermore, my car was only a year old; Laura's was only three years old. Three accidents and three breakdowns within a thirty-eight-day period seemed too many to be coincidental.

None of the accidents had been our fault. Although they appeared to be legitimate accidents, I wondered if all of them were. I questioned the timing of mine since it occurred immediately after examining military intervention with aliens. I wondered if someone other than an employee had loosened

124

the nuts on Laura's wheel while the car sat at the repair shop overnight. And the accident report revealed that Laura's second accident was caused by a young man employed by the Air Force. I wondered if military/government agents were trying to frighten me into abandoning further investigation of the alien phenomenon and were using my daughters in the process.

I would not yield to terrorism. I would not let guilt smother me. I did not want any of my family or friends to get hurt because of my investigations, and I intended to insulate them as much as possible. But if a military/government agent hurt them, the blood would be on his hands, not mine. I had the right to understand the alien phenomenon which had attacked my life, and I would let no one stop me from trying!

CHAPTER FOURTEEN

It would have been nice if I could have understood the strange incidents that had occurred since I began my quest into the alien phenomenon before experiencing any new ones. But such was not the case. Unexplained events continued throughout the fall of 1991.

On the night of August 14, I had an uneasy feeling when I went to bed. I usually am unable to sleep with lights glaring in my eyes. But this night I felt an inexplicable need to leave the bathroom light on so it would shine dimly into my bedroom. At approximately 2:00 a.m., the light went out. Thinking the bulb had shot, I climbed out of bed and turned on another light. I immediately heard an owl hooting as soon as I climbed back into bed.

I had heard this owl sound many times since moving into our new home. There was something disturbing about it. It sounded mechanical, not quite real. It reminded me of a duck caller my dad used for hunting; the sound that came from it was similar to a duck, but not quite the same. The sound of my mechanical owl tonight made me even more uneasy, keeping me awake until well after 5:00 a.m. When I finally arose at 7:00 a.m., I discovered the light that had gone out during the night was now mysteriously working.

On August 16, I noticed a window in the sun room was unlocked and the screen loose. No family members or guests had touched the window and no one had a clue as to who had tampered with it.

During the same week as the light and window incidents, I crossed paths three times with a strange-looking man. I could not remember where I first saw him. The second time was at the post office. The third time was at a fast-food restaurant on the other side of town. Each time I saw him, he was alone and appeared to be doing nothing other than watching people. I felt uneasy when he looked at me. I felt compelled to go up and speak to him, but something held me back. He was very thin, about six feet tall and approximately 60 years old. Like the mechanical owl, there was something unreal about him. He looked almost hollow. I told myself that in all probability he was simply a lonely man with an incurable disease. Yet, his presence unnerved me, as if he could see all the way into my soul.

The weekend of August 23, Mike and I went to New Orleans. While Mike attended a continuing education seminar Saturday morning, I lingered over croissants and hot chocolate while enjoying the view of the river from our room. I brushed my teeth and started back toward the windows to watch a boat pass by. Suddenly I felt something protruding from my gum behind my bottom front teeth. Raking my tongue across it, I felt something like a bone or chip of tooth sticking out. I raked my tongue over the area several times but could not dislodge the object. Finally I raked my fingernail hard across my gum, and it came out. It looked like a flat piece of brass, square except for one small corner missing. Mike entered the room as I examined it.

"What *is* this?" I asked him.

"It looks like a computer chip," he answered. "Where did you get it?"

"From my mouth. Have you ever seen a computer chip?"

"No," he admitted, "except in magazines. What was it doing in your mouth?"

I did not know. What the object was and how it had gotten there were a mystery. I mailed the object to John Carpenter for his opinion. He promised to have it analyzed.

During the night of August 27, noises that sounded like footsteps on the oak stairs awakened me. At first I thought that perhaps Laura or Kelly was up, but when I heard a door open and close, I sat up in bed rigid with fear. Soft, unidentifiable noises echoed through the house. An hour later the doorbell to the sun room rang. I was still too frightened to get out of bed until morning when I heard Laura and Kelly stirring. Both of them denied getting up during the night. I shuddered as I recalled my similar experience the night of July 1.

For weeks I had trouble sleeping because I kept thinking about the unexplained events taking place. I had difficulty breathing after my traffic accident; the pressure of the seatbelt

128

restraint had caused internal swelling in my chest. And I had been having pain near my temples since July, not long after I suspected the shock treatment had taken place. Now I was mentally and physically exhausted. Insufficient sleep and my weakened physical condition were taking a toll on me. I knew I could not continue to function in this condition. I told myself that I could no longer worry about what aliens or military/government agents were doing; I had to get some sleep.

Although it had taken more than a year, I finally accepted the reality of both the alien and military abductions explored under hypnosis, and I did decide to write a book about them. I was untrained as a writer, yet I was being badgered by the aliens' directive to *spread the word*. A gnawing force inside convinced me it was part of my responsibility to heed these instructions.

By September 27, I had completed the first draft of chapter one. I discussed this project with no one over the phone. I wrote a letter to John about my project. And I discussed it with Mike and Seth, but only in my home and through letters.

On October 1, I received a strange call on the phone in our bedroom. I couldn't tell whether the voice on the other end was male or female, and I couldn't determine whether the person was asking for Laura or Lauren. I asked the person to repeat three times whom the call was for, but Mike accidentally disconnected us when he picked up an extension to turn on the security system. The caller did not phone again.

An hour and a half later, Mike and I were sitting in the office discussing the pseudonyms I had chosen for my book and the progress I had made. The office phone rang and a distinctly female voice asked for Seth. I immediately made the connection between the two calls: Laura, Seth—both were pseudonyms I was using. I doubted the phone calls were coincidental. Craston is such a small town that few, if any, Seths live there. Furthermore, the phone number in our bedroom is unlisted and rarely results in wrong numbers.

But what was the purpose of the phone calls? Was it merely to inform me that someone knew about my book and I had no secrets? How did the individual acquire information concerning my writing? Had someone read my mail? Had someone been in my house and read my rough drafts? Was there a monitoring device in my house? Whatever method was used, I resented the invasion of privacy.

During the nights of October 2 and 7, someone or something turned off the security system during the night. I had turned it on myself and double-checked it before going to sleep, yet the next morning it was off. Laura, Kelly, and I had not touched it. I wondered whether aliens or military/government agents were responsible. If humans were trying to frighten me, they were certainly succeeding.

Another frightening episode occurred on Friday evening, October 11, when I was home alone. Mike had not come home for the weekend, and Laura and Kelly were at their high school football game. While washing dishes in the kitchen, I heard noises in the vicinity of the stairs or upstairs balcony. I became frightened but told myself they were probably normal house sounds and I was simply being too jumpy. As soon as I finished the dishes, I went upstairs. I locked my bedroom door behind me. I walked through the master suite into the bathroom and began brushing my teeth. I heard an extremely loud noise in the hall outside my bedroom. This time I knew it could not be a normal house noise. I ran out of the bathroom, jumped on my bed, and phoned Mike. While we were talking, I heard what sounded like someone trying to turn my doorknob. Rigid with fear, I bluffed by loudly announcing that if anyone came through the door, I would blow heads off first and ask questions later. Soon I heard softer, unidentifiable sounds I supposed came from someone creeping down the stairs. Mike talked with me until I calmed down and felt safe. Still, I was too frightened to move and remained alert on my bed for hours until Laura and Kelly came home. Then I opened my bedroom door and found the grid that covered the air return lying in the hall outside my bedroom. I looked inside the air return, stunned to discover that the area was large enough to stand inside. Apparently, someone had hidden there. I eliminated the possibility of a robber because nothing was stolen. And if the intruder were a murderer or rapist, why not commit the crime upon first entering the house instead of hiding in the air return? I concluded the intruder must have been a military/government agent. What did these people want? Did they simply intend to frighten me, or were their intentions more malign?

On October 18, I flew to St. Louis for a MUFON conference. Mike took a separate flight and arrived late that night. He had a case of diarrhea that weakened him so much he had intravenous fluids administered at the hospital earlier that day. I asked him why he came to the conference when he was so ill. He explained he thought government agents were responsible for his illness. He felt they were trying to prevent him from attending the conference, and he was determined not to let them succeed. We wondered whether my intruder of October 11 also had intended to make me too ill to attend the conference. We probably will never know if our suspicions were warranted.

Mike remained in bed throughout most of the conference while John and I met privately with a group of ufologists to discuss my experiences with military/government agents. The group was attentive and supportive as they listened to my story. When our meeting was over, I felt safer knowing that these UFO investigators shared all the important secrets I possessed.

Mike remained ill for several weeks after the conference; I was extremely worried about him as his illness had led to internal bleeding. His doctor diagnosed the problem as a severe bacterial infection. Because the illness was bacterial rather than viral and because of its timing, Mike felt more certain than ever that he was a victim of foul play.

I was a victim of several physical anomalies during the fall. In July, while in Springfield, Missouri, I had experienced spasms in my lower back. I was sitting on the bed in my hotel room when they hit. At first I thought something was shaking the bed. I got up and looked under it but saw nothing. Again the spasms hit and I realized that the shaking was in my back, not from an external force. Then in September the spasms reoccurred several times. I wondered if these spasms could be a result of the medical procedures performed on me by my human abductors. The thought angered me.

On the morning of October 25, I discovered a small scratch on my left wrist that was bleeding slightly and a yellow-green bruise approximately an inch away from it. There also was a brown, oval-shaped brand on my neck. It looked as if someone had taken a small cookie cutter and pressed it into my skin. By noon, the brand had disappeared. During the afternoon, I began to feel as if I had been scraped inside. These physical symptoms led me to believe that an abduction encounter had taken place during the night, but I could remember nothing about it. I became angry at my abductors. Why wouldn't they allow me to remember my encounters? Why?

I suspected another encounter the night of October 28. I woke up the next morning with an extremely sore right nostril. High inside, near my eye, I felt as if a foreign object had been inserted. It was uncomfortable; I wanted to get it out. But it was too far inside to be reached.

On November 14, I discovered a new scar hidden in my hair above my right temple. The scar was small, white, and jagged. I knew it had not been there long, but I did not know exactly what date it appeared. Nor did I know what caused it.

One autumn weekend Mike discovered three strange marks on my back where the skin was bruised and indented. The indentations were almost rectangular, approximately three fourths of an inch long and one half of an inch wide. My schedule was hectic during October and November, so I failed to document the exact date Mike found them. I knew only that they appeared during one of those months. They remained for several weeks.

On November 23, Mike and I drove to Fort Walton Beach and Gulf Breeze to see if we could find any evidence related to my beach incident. We came back home disappointed. We learned that the Joint Chiefs of Staff met at Pensacola Naval Air Station in August, 1988, and were escorted into a hangar that was under extremely high security and temporarily air conditioned. We also learned that on November 21, 1988, some teenagers were told by Air Force personnel to leave the Gulf Islands National Seashore because there was an incident in progress. But these details alone were not enough to satisfy me.

On December 4, I noticed that my computer diskettes were out of order and two-thirds of the last letter I had written to John had been erased. No one in our household was responsible for this. Of course, I was resentful that some unknown person had been tampering with my personal belongings. And I was frustrated over my inability to exercise control over these strange incidents that left me baffled as to their purpose.

CHAPTER FIFTEEN

Not only was autumn filled with perplexing incidents, it also was filled with more alien-related dreams and odd mental flashes.

On August 25, 1991, I dreamed I felt an alien force pulling me out of bed and I pleaded, "Please not tonight. I'm too tired." An alien telepathically replied, "This is necessary. We must fill your mind with more knowledge." Then symbols rapidly started flowing through my head.

When I awoke, I remembered only one of the symbols, the symbol for man. The dream was so vivid and evoked so much emotion I decided it was probably an actual event.

The next evening I discussed the episode over the phone with a well-known MUFON investigator. She asked if I had seen any helicopters flying around my house lately. I told her I hadn't. But at 2:14 a.m. that very night, the sound of a loud helicopter flying directly over my bedroom awakened me. Was the helicopter chasing away a spaceship? Had the military listened in on my phone conversation and thought that since the aliens had visited me the night before they might come back this night? Was the helicopter merely a message that the military was listening to my phone conversations? I knew the helicopter was there for some specific reason since helicopters typically did not fly directly over my house, especially in the middle of the night.

For the next few nights, I was able to sleep undisturbed. Then on August 31, I had another vivid dream. I was looking at Earth from a distance. To her left, I saw another planet move toward and then merge with Earth. As I witnessed this event, an alien explained I am being prepared for the related changes that will take place as a result of this future merging.

When I awoke and thought about this dream, I realized the only dreams I could ever remember in detail dealt with spaceships or aliens or abductions by military-type humans. I had dreamed about tornadoes many times, but I never could remember details about them once I woke up. Perhaps my vivid dreams were more significant than I had realized and I should pay more attention to them in the future.

My first chance came on September 23 when I dreamed I was examining a pear. I studied not only the exterior but also the cellular structure beneath the skin. When I awoke, I thought, "Why did I dream about the cellular structure of a pear? I have very little interest in science."

Suddenly a silent voice said to me, "This is part of your instruction." I accepted this as confirmation that I should pay more attention to these vivid dreams.

On September 25, I was plagued by mental images again after reading my Bible and praying. I saw tiny veins on green leaves; tiny creatures resembling sperm; a round, porous, wheat-colored, sponge-like object; and charcoal-colored material resembling clay. Next I saw a life form that looked as if it were part plant, part spider. Finally I saw a normal-looking spider that was dead and brittle. Big black ants crawled over it and died.

What was happening to me? Were these images part of my instruction, too? I felt if the aliens were trying to teach me something about science, they certainly had a sense of humor; I didn't know the difference between a cell and a molecule.

Several mental flashes that occurred during the fall were apparently pieces of surfacing memory. I remembered walking into a hotel lobby, wearing an overcoat that did not belong to me. I remembered one of my human captors had an eagle on the arm of his uniform. And I remembered flying in a military airplane. I was glad I remembered these things but annoyed I could not remember the entire event from which they came.

I received another strange mental flash on October 2 after reading my Bible and praying. It was as if a silent voice was telling me to read page 29.

"What?" I thought, startled by this silent intrusion.

Again the message came, "Read page 29."

I envisioned the page of a book with the number "29" in the top right-hand margin. I could visualize words on the page, but I could not distinguish individual words.

"I can't read something I can't physically see," I argued.

But again the silent voice demanded, "Read page 29."

I realized the silent voice was going to badger me until I tried. After a great deal of effort, I could make out only a few words. The top paragraph said something about the family of God being transported away from Earth. The second paragraph said something about an odyssey.

When the page disappeared from my mind, I realized that of all the strange things that had happened to me, this was the strangest. Who had sent this message? How had it been sent? And why?

I shared this incident with several people at the MUFON conference in St. Louis. Rather than showing skepticism as I somewhat expected, they indicated they had heard of incidents such as this before. They seemed disappointed I had failed to intercept the entire message. Therefore, on October 30, when I was alone and everything was quiet, I decided to try to initiate telepathic communication with whomever or whatever tried to show me page 29. I didn't know if it would work. Furthermore, I worried I might be treading on ground that God intended us to avoid. I asked God to forgive me if I was going against His will. Then I began my contact. "I am willing to communicate with entities who love the Lord my God, who serve Him and worship Him as their one and only God," I said silently. "Someone recently asked me to read page 29 and I failed. I am willing to try again. This time I will put forth my best effort."

I waited, still and silent, for several minutes. Nothing happened. As I was beginning to feel my attempt was futile, a silent message rushed at me, "Do not worry about trying to read page 29. Get out some paper and a pen. We will paraphrase it for you."

Surprised to have received an answer, I did as I was told. The message came to me not in separate words, but in complete thoughts. They rushed into my head faster than I could write them down. When the communication stopped, I read what I had written:

> After these events have occurred as recorded, the family of God will be transported away from Earth to another universe. They are now being

prepared for the journey that is to take place. The Earth will meet with destruction, ignited by man. A total upheaval will occur. Chosen ones have been pre-selected to ensure their species' continued existence. They are being prepared for adaptation to their new environment.

There is much work to be done before the odyssey can take place. Time is of the essence. Faith is important. Faith is the reason not everyone knows. Belief in God is a prerequisite, not proof and not evidence. The family of God will be delivered from Earth by their cohorts. The odyssey is to take place swiftly and precipitously. The family of God know they're being prepared and are being given their instructions.

Astonished my attempt was successful, I pondered over these words. I wondered who had sent this message and from what book the material was taken. What did the first twenty-eight pages say? What type of destruction would Earth face? Where was this new environment? I knew only that I was one of the people being prepared and given instructions, and that the information was being stored to be brought into conscious memory at the right time. Contemplating these words, I wondered if somehow the key to the whole alien phenomenon lay within them.

In addition to these mental flashes, I had several more dreams during the fall of 1991. On October 9, I dreamed I was with a group of friends and relatives at the Gulf Coast. We were standing near the ocean as it began to get dark. I asked Mike if he would get our camera out of the car; I wanted to take pictures of UFOs if we saw any. While Mike was gone, one of my friends yelled at me to look up. As I was looking at an object I knew had to be a spaceship, a smaller object swooped down from the sky and, taking me by surprise, beamed me up to it. I was upset the aliens had snatched me away from my friends. I protested and started calling for Ceto. After a few seconds, the aliens told me their action was necessary, that I was being prepared for the transition.

On November 11, I dreamed I was resisting some kind of force pulling me out of bed. There was a loud, almost deafening, buzz in my right ear. I told whatever was present to go away and leave me alone, that I had to get up and go to work soon. I tried to move my arms and legs, but electrical currents shot through them. I managed to struggle out of bed with the currents continuing to shoot through me. Suddenly some sort of force scattered my belongings all over my room. I became angry that this force would have the audacity to mess up my room like that. Then the pain from the electrical currents became so excruciating I could no longer focus on anger. When the alarm clock awakened me, I gazed around the room, relieved to find everything was in its place.

On November 20, I dreamed I was near my bedroom window and saw my body lying on the bed. I noticed my eyes were closed, I had on no makeup, and I looked lifeless. When I awoke and remembered this dream, an eerie feeling overwhelmed me. I wondered if it was a memory of either an out-of-body or a near-death experience.

The next dream occurred the night of December 3. I dreamed I was outside and saw a large beam of white light in the sky, slanting leftward toward the ground. To the left of the beam, there were alternating pulses of orange and white light. Due to the location of the beam and pulsating lights, I knew there had to be two UFOs, but I could see neither of them. I soon found myself in the back seat of an unfamiliar car, taking pictures of a UFO that was obviously maneuvering itself so I could take pictures of it easily. When the UFO left, I saw an alien looking in the rear window of the car. He looked human except for his bronze-colored skin. He had brown hair, brushed straight back.

I awoke from this dream at 4:46 a.m. and heard an unidentifiable humming sound that lasted approximately twenty seconds and then disappeared abruptly. When I got up, I discovered the lock on my bedroom door was unbolted. I was one hundred percent certain I had bolted the door before going to bed. I had no idea how it had become unfastened.

The following weekend, I was describing the dream to Mike when Kelly came in and said, "Mom, I can tell you what night you had that dream, Tuesday night. I heard a humming sound at 12:30. I don't know how I knew, but I knew the sound was coming from a spaceship. I thought, 'They're probably here for Mom. I hope she has a pleasant journey!'"

Kelly was right; the dream did occur on Tuesday night. I was thankful Kelly had been unafraid when she suspected the presence of an alien craft and that she was able to find humor in the situation.

The next apparent encounter occurred during the night of December 19. I woke up at 2:26 a.m. and heard an interior door open and close. I fell back asleep almost immediately and dreamed I felt a force pulling me out of bed. I started floating toward my bedroom door and thought, "Here I go through the door like I have many times before. It's time for me to dematerialize now."

As I passed through the door, I noticed two pieces of notebook paper folded neatly, sticking out of the crack of the door. I removed them and began reading one. I saw it contained a full page of information I would not be able to finish before the force delivered me at my destination. I stuck that paper in the pocket of my robe and began reading the second one. It contained a strange kind of mathematical system, a way of counting that was different from ours. I felt as if the aliens were trying to teach me this new system. When I finished studying the page, I stuck it in my pocket along with the other.

Soon afterwards, I found myself walking toward what appeared to be a sea vessel docked at the edge of a body of water. I walked on board ship and found human-looking aliens working there. Since I had gone through this process many times, I merely asked them if they were ready for me. Someone indicated they were, so I walked to a table and lay down. I asked a female alien who seemed to be in charge whether people other than abductees ever wandered aboard ship, and if so, who they thought the aliens were. The answer I received had something to do with disciples. Then a Doberman appeared at my right side. I told the alien I was afraid of big dogs, and I asked her to get it away from me. The dog started gnawing on the right side of my body. I became terrified but knew I shouldn't move. Finally the alien told the dog to go away. My side hurt where the dog had taken two chunks out of it.

I woke up from this dream at 3:20 a.m. My left temple

hurt for a few seconds; then my right temple hurt for the same length of time. I immediately picked up a notepad and began writing down my dream because I was afraid I would forget it. At 3:42 a.m. I heard what sounded like a small motor in the woods. It sounded as if it might be a chain saw or gas-powered hedge clippers or a lawn mower. I thought, "Who in the world would be doing yard work in the middle of the night when it's pitch black dark?" It made no sense. When I climbed out of bed several hours later, I searched the pockets of my robe for folded notebook paper. Disappointed, but not surprised, I found none there.

During December I received an additional message from the silent voice. It said, "Get rid of all worry, fear, and anger. They create mind noise."

I knew exactly what that message meant. For a long time I had felt intense fear that military/government agents might kill me or one of my family members because I had interpreted all their actions as overt threats. But even greater than my fear was the anger I felt toward them. They had no right to keep the public ignorant of the alien phenomenon. They especially had no right to keep pertinent information from people they knew were personally affected by the phenomenon.

And, yes, I was filled with worry. Worry about financial problems. Worry about the effect my involvement in the alien phenomenon was having on my family. Worry that it was beginning to be too much for Mike to deal with and he would leave me. Worry that I might be caught up in something so evil I could never escape it. Worry that my involvement in the phenomenon might cost me my job. In essence, I worried about every aspect of my life that I considered important.

This worry, fear, and anger had been consuming my thoughts, cluttering my mind. I knew the silent voice was telling me it had trouble getting through to me when I allowed these negative emotions to fill my mind. I also knew the silent voice was telling me I needed to rid myself of these negative emotions for my own sake, that they were smothering me somehow. I knew it would be hard to cast them out, but I made a silent vow to try.

Although I perfectly understood this last telepathic message, the other mental flashes and dreams that emerged during the fall continued to be perplexing. Again I decided to return to Springfield in the hope I would gain some insight into what had become an ever-expanding puzzle.

CHAPTER SIXTEEN

I went back to Springfield the first week of January, 1992. This time Mike accompanied me. He requested the first hypnosis session to see whether he had experienced any abductions. But because Mike would not allow himself to relax completely, his session with John was unsuccessful.

The next session was reserved for me. John hooked up the microphone and began. "January 3, 1991," he said.

"1992," I corrected him.

"Yeah, thank you," John said. "Wrong year. See, you're oriented. No one will lock you up."

John, Grace, and I first discussed flashes of memory, including the telepathic image of my "son," and dreams I had experienced since my last visit. John seemed particularly interested in my dream of December 3 in which I took pictures of a spaceship, especially when I told him there were seven pictures on my roll of film no one could remember taking. I explained that when I had the film developed, the first seven pictures did not come out.

Finally we were ready for hypnosis. After the relaxation process, John asked me to recall snapping pictures and to describe what I saw in the viewfinder. I remembered focusing on a huge spaceship when a blinding light engulfed me. A thin, wise-looking creature, taller than Ceto's race, stood facing me in the light, gesturing as he instructed me. I knew he was teaching me something as part of my preparation for the future, but I could not remember what. Our entire conversation was telepathic. When my teacher finished the instruction, he said, "Go now." I could remember nothing further about this incident.

Next John asked me to recall a time when I was in a hotel lobby. I remembered standing in a back area of the lobby near the elevators wearing a dark-colored overcoat that did not belong to me. The sleeves were too long and were annoying me. Two men had brought me into the hotel. While one went to the desk to get a key to my room, the other stood next to me with a gun in his pocket and told me I had better not try anything. I was resentful and angry at being treated like a prisoner, but I was too frightened to make a scene and so obeyed my captor. As we waited for the key, I noticed the restaurant employees setting up the breakfast buffet. When the other man returned, we went up to my room.

John asked me to back up in time and remember what took place before we arrived at the hotel. I remembered riding in the back seat of a big blue car, feeling dazed, but no conversation other than one of the men saying, "Remember what we told you. Don't try anything."

John asked me to back up in time again to the first time I caught sight of the car. I remembered coming down steps from an airplane. A man behind me ordered me to get into the car. I was not allowed to look around. I could not remember how, when, or where I got on the plane or anything about being inside it, not even the flight. I could remember only getting off the plane.

John asked me to go forward in time again and to remember what happened once the men and I went up to my hotel room. I remembered Mike was supposed to be inside. One of the men opened the door and went inside. The other kept me outside in the hall. Standing with my back against the wall, I began to feel dizzy. The last thing I could remember about this incident was slithering down the wall into the floor as everything around me turned black.

John told me to change scenes, to drift through time and focus on an image of a little boy with brown hair. I remembered being aboard a spaceship and being shown something like a three-dimensional video of the child. The video appeared in front of my face after the creatures extracted ova from me. A creature standing to my right told me the child is my son. They wanted me to know what they had done with some of my eggs.

Next I remembered standing outside a windowed partition and viewing what I called a "baby greenhouse." On the other side of the partition was a room filled with transparent containers suspended in the air. A part-alien, part-human baby was suspended in each container. They looked like fetuses with chalky-colored skin, big heads, and no hair. I was amazed at the intensity of the light in the room; it seemed much too bright for babies. Somehow I knew that again I was being shown how the creatures were using my eggs. Since my memory ended there, John ended the session.

Later, when I was alone, I thought about these incidents. I wondered what instructions the teacher gave me in the light and when the time would come for me to use them. I wondered if the incident in the hotel lobby was related to the crash at the beach. If it wasn't, why had I been on an airplane? Where had I been? What had happened before and during the flight?

I wondered where the little boy with brown hair was now and how many babies in the nursery belonged to me. Would I ever see them again? What about their paternity? At least I felt certain they were being well cared for, and although I didn't understand how I knew it, I felt comfort in knowing they were better off with the creatures than with me.

But again I was disappointed, as the session had produced so many new questions and so few answers.

CHAPTER SEVENTEEN

For the next session, John decided to allow my mind to roam freely and explore whatever it wished. Unaccustomed to being given this type of freedom in a session, I found it difficult to sort through events and arrive at one that seemed more important than others. And it was very difficult to get anything focused sufficiently in my mind.

After a great deal of effort, I found myself looking out the entrance of a building encased in a hillside. The opening was large, similar to a garage door. I saw a blue sky, men in green fatigues, and a jeep. Then I saw a black helicopter fly over. The facility was dimly lit and had a flat ceiling. A man in green fatigues and a strange-looking creature stood near the entrance to my left. The creature was short, not much higher than the knees of the man.

"I'm not supposed to remember this," I announced to John and Grace.

"You can always forget later," John assured me. "But now you can remember. What else about the little creature?"

"He has dark eyes, but rounded. They're not like those of the other creatures. I remember his strange hair." I paused. "I'm not supposed to remember this," I repeated.

"What about the hair?" John pressed.

"It's matted down in the back of his head. I don't see any hair from the front."

"What color?" John asked.

"It's like the color of his skin."

"And what color is that?"

"Kind of...I'm not supposed to remember," I said, stopping myself. "I know I'm not."

"Who tells you not to remember?" John wanted to know.

"I don't know," I replied.

John asked me several more times about the skin color, but I couldn't remember it. Next I remembered lying on a table underneath a light. I was unable to keep my eyes open because of the brightness. The light sometimes had a reddish tint like a heat lamp.

"What do you remember now?" John asked.

"I feel dizzy as if I had some tranquilizers or something," I mumbled.

"Do you hear anything?" John asked.

"Somebody asks me questions," I replied.

"What kind of questions?"

"I don't remember the specific questions. I'm not supposed to remember. I'm told I'll be punished."

"Who will punish you?" John wondered.

I could not remember who specifically would be responsible for my punishment. "It's like an echo," I continued. "It's like an echo of the words, 'You will be punished.' Like an echo over and over and over."

"You will *not* be punished," John assured me. "That's a false threat. You will not be punished. It's just a scare tactic. It's safe to remember now." He paused. "What's one question they ask you?"

"They wanted to know what the aliens did to me on the spaceship," I replied.

"What do you say?"

"I don't answer."

"What do they say next?"

I felt something like intense electrical currents shoot through my body. "They do something to make my body hurt when I don't answer," I replied. "I feel it all over."

"Does that cause you to answer their questions?" John asked.

"He asked me again, 'Tell us what happens to you when you're aboard the spaceship.' I still don't answer."

"And then what happens?" John wanted to know.

"Pain again," I said, feeling intense shock flow through my body.

"Do you feel any pressure or touch anywhere?"

"I'm strapped down. I don't feel anything except the pain when they ask a question and I refuse to answer."

"Why don't you answer? Do you like the pain?" John asked.

"No, it's horrible!" I replied.

"Do you know the answer to what he asks?" John questioned. "What could you have told them about what the creatures did on the craft?"

"I could tell them about the creatures scraping tissue samples from the vaginal area and extracting ova with the needle and putting them in the black box and — "

"Why didn't you tell them?" John interrupted.

"I don't know. I don't remember."

"What else could you have told them but didn't?"

"Lots of things. Like what it looks like to look out the window at Earth."

"What are the windows like?" John asked.

"Real thick with a bluish tint," I answered. "I could have told them how the creatures communicate, what the implants are for," I added.

"What do you know about that?" John wondered.

"The ear implants are for communicating and monitoring," I explained. "They can signal the aliens when we're in trouble, and the aliens can communicate through those waves when they're not present but need to talk to us. But I don't tell the man anything."

"Why are you so loyal to the aliens?" John wanted to know.

"Because they're trying to help us," I told him. "We can't continue to survive on Earth without their help."

"So why all the secrecy?" John wondered.

"They can't save everyone," I explained. "They can't save us all."

"How do they know who to save?" John asked.

"I don't know."

"So you told them none of this," John mused. "But you saw a creature with them, so they would know all this already."

"No," I explained. "He's not the same kind."

I remembered the creature's uniform. It was a blue, one-piece uniform made from material resembling felt, a red sash tied around the waist, a red emblem on the arm. Somehow I got the impression the alien was the one who administered the shock when I refused to answer their questions, but I could see him only out of the corner of my eye. I remembered his mouth was a small slit, but I never remembered him communicating in any way.

Next I remembered standing outside. The sky was bright blue with fluffy white clouds. The day was sunny and warm. The rolling hills nearby were green with vegetation. A man in a jeep looked through binoculars at the sky. I looked up, too, and saw three black helicopters emerge from behind the hill the facility was housed in and fly away from us. I felt dazed as I stood there looking at the action, oblivious, void of emotion. I could remember nothing further, so John ended the session.

The short alien I remembered in this session was the same type that appeared in both dreams I had in July, 1991, the dreams in which a creature attached a scope to my body and in which a creature accompanied humans inside a man-made craft. There was something odd about this creature, something mystical, almost unreal, but I could not pinpoint exactly what it was. I knew, however, I didn't like him and I hoped I would never run into him again.

My principal question after considering the material that emerged during the session was when and where this incident took place. I knew it had occurred during the daytime. Since I had never inexplicably missed any of my classes or a day of work, I concluded it must have taken place at a time when I was not working or going to graduate school. And it seemed it would have been at a time when my husband was at work and my daughters were in school.

I thought back to the spring of 1988 in Tennessee when I was self-employed and prepared tax returns in my home. One weekday that spring the time seemed to have just slipped away. Also during that spring, for several days, I broke into tears without knowing why. I could find no logical explanation for either mystery. So now I wondered if my visit to the hillside facility occurred during that time frame. If so, then the military/government knew about my involvement with the aliens before I moved to Craston. Before I ever wrote the first letter to Budd Hopkins. Even before I told anyone about my dreams concerning aliens.

I wondered just how long they had known about it. I wondered if they had been monitoring me for many years, even throughout my entire lifetime, without my knowledge. And I wondered if perhaps they had given the aliens permission to abduct me.

CHAPTER EIGHTEEN

The next night, once John had me in the hypnotic state, he simply asked me to recall a recent incident that had disturbed my sleep.

I recalled I awoke to find Ceto, my alien friend, standing next to my bed. I got up and unquestioningly went with him as I had many times before. He took my hand and we floated through the air, through the bedroom door, down the stairs, and through the front door. Standing outside, I saw a spaceship at treetop level. At first it looked like an orange ball of light. Then it changed to white and then back to orange again.

"What do you do when you see it?" John asked.

"We're waiting for the beam of light," I explained.

"What kind of light is this?" John asked.

"Just white light," I replied, "like little sunrays all together. Kind of like fog. We just stand there and it beams us up. Now I'm standing in a round room in the spaceship."

"Have you seen this room before?" John asked.

"Yeah."

"Describe it."

"It's rounded all over. Totally. I see blinking red and white lights inside the wall of the spaceship." I paused. "Strange! I don't feel the floor beneath me!"

"Do you see a floor?" John asked.

"Not really," I replied. "It's strange."

"Are you alone in this room?" John wanted to know.

"No. There are four creatures."

"What happens now?"

"I'm lying down on the platform I'm always on. There's the black machine above me. They lower it, and a needle comes out and goes into my right ovary. It hurts real badly. They're taking eggs out and putting them in the black box."

"What else do they do?" John asked.

"I have to close my eyes," I replied. "They're doing something with my right eye. It seems like they're reconstructing the whole thing. It doesn't hurt, but I feel pressure."

"Do they have tools, or are they using their fingers?" John asked.

"I can't see," I answered. "I have my eyes shut. I feel as if I've been sedated, but I'm aware."

"So it doesn't really bother you that much?" John asked.

"It doesn't last long. They're through."

"Did you receive any communication about what they were doing?" John wondered.

"To see colors more clearly," I told him. "My nose feels different, too. When they get through with my eye, it feels as if there's something in there."

"What do you notice about your nose?" John asked.

"When they're messing with my eye, it feels as if they're inserting an object into my nose. But they don't do it from the nostril; they put it in from the eye area. It feels like they pressed it into the inside of my nose, like they were fusing it. It feels as if it's attached inside. I don't know how they do it."

"And is it a bloody mess?" John wondered.

"No," I said. "It doesn't bleed. But after they take the eye out and put the object in and put the eye back in, my nose hurts."

"What do they tell you about that?" John asked.

"I don't remember. It has to do with adaptation to a future environment."

John changed the subject. "You've gotten flashes of things at times about a purpose, a mission, a teaching, a learning, page 29, and all these things you're supposed to be taught and instructed. Maybe some of that can come forward clearly now." John paused. "What have you learned?"

"They're storing information in lots of us," I replied. "We know who we are. We can't survive without this reservoir of information. We'll need it all, but we don't need it yet. We'll need it a little at a time."

"How do you know these are their words and not your own thoughts?" John wanted to know.

"They've explained it," I answered. "That's what he told me in the light."

"Who told you?"

"The teacher."

After the teacher vanished from my memory, I remembered seeing what I described as "an angel-like man" standing in a light. He was tall, with long blonde hair and blue eyes. A long white robe stood out against his tan-colored skin. There was an aura about him; beauty and kindness radiated from him. He told me to pay attention to the messages they send and to obey the teacher, to learn from him, that it was very important. Like all the other creatures I had encountered, he spoke with his eyes rather than with his mouth. When he finished speaking, he vanished instantly. I was left alone in a light beam. My next memory was of being back home in bed.

"Being in bed?" John asked. "All right. How did your door once get unbolted?"

"I unbolted it."

"Why did you unbolt the door? There must have been a good reason for you to unbolt the door which kept you safe. What causes you to get up?"

"There's a light shining in the window," I replied. "I'm going to take a picture of it. I run fast and get the camera from the office. I go back in the bedroom and turn off the alarm. I run down the stairs, unlock the front door, and run out. I see orange and white pulsating above the trees. I take pictures of it. First it's an orange ball, then a white ball. That's strange! It changes shapes! The shape is different. The color is different."

"What shape do you see now?" John asked.

"Like two convergent saucers. Silver. I don't understand how it can change colors and shapes. It doesn't make sense. They know I'm taking pictures. It's like they're doing a performance for me."

"How bright are the lights?" John inquired.

"The orange light and the white light are very bright. When it changes to a metallic saucer, it's not bright at all. I can barely see the outline. It's got blue on it. Like a silver, metallic, but with a blue cast to it. And blue portholes around it."

"What happens after you take pictures?"

"I don't remember. The last thing I remember is taking pictures."

"But now you remember how the door got unbolted," John

remarked. "And the seven pictures on your film you couldn't explain."

John brought me out of hypnosis at that point. I adamantly stated I did not consciously recall taking seven pictures of spacecraft.

"Did you or did you not have seven pictures on a roll of film that could not be explained by anybody?" John argued.

"Yes, but ..." I left the sentence unfinished because I could not explain how the pictures had gotten there.

Unfortunately, the pictures had not turned out when I had the film developed, so there was no proof as to what had been on those seven frames. To think that I could have had some evidence of an encounter with UFOs! I was so upset over this possible loss that I could think of very little else until my hypnosis session the next night.

CHAPTER NINETEEN

When John and Grace met me for the next hypnosis session, I told them that during hypnosis the previous night I remembered looking out a blue porthole and seeing the ocean below. I had failed to mention this memory at the time because I simultaneously remembered the incident concerning my eye and we explored that instead. Tonight, after John put me under, he asked me to recall what I saw through the porthole.

I remembered the water being a beautiful blue color as we floated slowly toward it. Two of the familiar black-eyed aliens stood on each side of me. At first they watched me, then they concentrated on blinking lights on a panel of the ship's wall. When we fell beneath the water's surface, I saw shadows, but I could not determine what the shadowy images represented. Then blackness filled the porthole, and I could no longer see out.

Next I remembered being in a dark parking garage filled with about a dozen spaceships. I could tell there were different types, but because the room was so dark, it was difficult to make out all the distinct shapes. I could see one was shaped like two convergent saucers with portholes around it and another looked almost round, a slight dome at the top and bottom.

"So where are you?" John asked.

"In the ocean somewhere."

"So it must be wet," John said.

"No," I replied. "It's not wet here."

"What's the ground like?" John asked.

"Hard-packed sand." I paused. "Why are they showing me these things? I don't understand why they're showing me these things. It's like different cars on a car lot. Like a fleet. Different ones for different purposes."

"Do you see water anywhere?" John asked.

"No."

"Do you see the ship you arrived on?"

"No. I'm not looking at it."

"But you got out of it, right?"

"Yeah, off the ramp. Four little guys follow me out. I don't know where they go. There's a door in the wall. It opens automatically. Somebody's there. Somebody went in that door. I caught a glimpse of a man dressed in green fatigues. It's shut now. I'm walking toward it. I don't know where that door goes. It's sort of like black metal. I'm close to that door now."

"As you stand by the door, what else do you notice?" John asked.

"The walls and ceiling are made of a strange material," I replied.

"Is it soft?"

"I don't remember touching it."

"What color?"

"A light reddish-brown color. It looks kind of like sea sponge material."

"Do you feel like you're under somebody's control?"

"No. It's like they want me to feel free to explore."

"That's odd, isn't it?" John asked.

"No," I replied matter-of-factly.

"So now what happens?" John asked.

"I'm in the room with the man. There's nothing in that room. Nothing at all. It's like a prison."

"So how do you get out of there?" John wondered.

"I just walk out the door."

"They're just letting you walk around and see all this?"

"Right."

"Why?"

"They want me to know that man is a prisoner," I explained. "I don't know why they want me to know. I just walk out that door, but the man has to stay there. I don't know why he's a prisoner."

"So how do you get out of there?" John asked.

"I go back up the same ramp. When I get inside the ship, I sit down in a weird kind of seat. I don't see any legs holding it up."

John jumped to another incident. "Remember a time when you dreamed you were on a table and a big dog came toward you."

154

I couldn't remember a dog; I could remember only people. "I don't know who that woman is," I said. "I don't know what they're doing to me. It looks like I'm in a hospital room."

"What makes it look like a hospital room?" John asked.

"The white uniform," I replied as I remembered catching a glimpse of a woman. "Yeah, she's a nurse or a doctor; I don't know which."

"Look at her face and see how she looks," John requested.

"No! She has black stripes on her shoulder," I discovered upon closer examination. "She looks like a female sailor."

"A female sailor," John repeated. "Does anybody call her a name?"

"Patty [pseudonym]," I replied.

"What does Patty do?" John asked.

"She takes my pulse," I replied. "I don't know where this is. This is confusing."

"What else does she do?"

"Blood pressure. Looks in my eyes with a light."

"What do her eyes look like?" John wanted to know.

"I don't remember what color they are."

"Human-looking eyes?"

"Oh, yeah, she's human. She has short, light brown hair."

"What else does she do?"

"She starts to argue with a man in the room. She says, 'You shouldn't have said my name, *Marvin* [pseudonym].' But I get the impression that's not his real name."

"Do you see him?" John asked.

"Yeah. He has short brown hair." I paused. "I'm getting dizzy now."

"Did they do something to you?" John asked.

"It's a shot in my right arm. It hurts."

"And then you start getting dizzy?"

"Yeah."

"Do you pass out?" John asked.

"I don't know. I can barely see that man. He has on a khaki-colored uniform."

"What does he say?"

"I don't remember."

"How did you get to this room?"

"I don't know. I don't know where I am."

"Is it a hospital that you recognize?" John wondered.

"I'm not sure it's a hospital room," I explained. "That's what I think at first when I see her uniform. But I'm not really sure where I am."

John ended the hypnosis session at that point. I was extremely upset at not remembering more. I had no clues as to when, where, and under what circumstances this last incident took place.

And who was the man who seemed to be a prisoner under the ocean? Why was he there and how long had he been there? Was he truly a prisoner? I wondered if he had been involved in the military cover-up of the alien phenomenon. I wondered if he had been partly responsible for my own problems resulting from my investigations. Was that why the aliens took me down there? To show me they sometimes punish those who torment their abductees? I hoped not. I thought about the bleakness, the emptiness of the underwater facility. I wouldn't wish such desolation on anyone.

Yes, I was angry at what military/government agents had done to me. Very angry. But I harbored no hostility toward the military or government in general; my complaint was against the elite within those organizations who were responsible for suppressing the truth about the alien phenomenon and for my related problems. To vent my hostility, I had invented a derogatory term that I used to describe this group, "OMAGS," for "obnoxious military and government scoundrels." Still, I wasn't interested in revenge. I only wanted them to stop interfering with my life and to let the public in on what they knew about the alien phenomenon.

Perhaps I had misinterpreted the situation in the underwater facility and the man in military fatigues wasn't a prisoner. But then, why was he down there? Something else occurred to me. I was alone in the room with that man for a while. Surely a conversation took place. What did we say to each other? And why couldn't I remember it?

I wished John could take me back to that room in another session to see if a conversation did indeed take place. But tomorrow I would have to go back home, not knowing when I would have the opportunity to undergo regressive hypnosis again.

EPILOGUE

My various experiences in the eighteen months from July 8, 1990, to January 7, 1992, have resulted in an upheaval of my life. The memories previously locked in the closets of my mind have forced me, sometimes kicking and screaming along the way, to expand my concept of reality and to open up the possibilities of even greater expansion.

Although many dreams and flashbacks remain unexplored and hundreds of questions remain unanswered, I have not yet undergone additional sessions of hypnotic regression. I probably will at some point, but I have concentrated on dealing with what I have uncovered so far. It hasn't been easy.

Analysis of the object that emerged from my gum in August, 1991, was completed in May, 1992. Photographs were taken using a scanning electron microscope. An energy dispersive spectroscopy scan also was done. The data suggested that the material was approximately 80% copper and 20% zinc, with small traces of aluminum and silicon. The object weighed approximately 6 milligrams. It was roughly 0.16cm square and 0.03cm thick. It did not react to a magnetic field and showed no radioactivity. In essence, the analysis showed that the material was consistent with common brass.

Later examination of hotel receipts indicated the incident in which two armed men brought me back to my hotel room probably occurred in August, 1988.

I have not heard from Captain Pugh since he appeared outside my classroom on May 6, 1991. Not surprisingly, no one has issued a second invitation for me to view a space shuttle. Because I adamantly refused to teach future classes at the Air Force Base, I was dismissed from my job after finishing the spring semester of 1992.

My husband's concern over financial costs at the onset of my investigation was justified. The trips to Springfield for

hypnosis sessions and telephone calls and postage to investigators and fellow abductees cost thousands of dollars just in
the first year. I prefer to keep my financial matters private,
but being a CPA, I feel a responsibility to warn abductees who
are considering undergoing hypnosis for the first time that
they should consider the financial aspects of their search as
well as the emotional ones.

One of the positive results of my alien contacts is that I no
longer allow fear, anger, and worry to control my life. Sometimes my human limitations cause me to backslide temporarily, but I know as long as I keep my focus on God, everything will be all right in the end. Ovary probes by the aliens
and torture by the OMAGS can at the very most destroy my
body. But I have learned my body is only a container for my
soul and they cannot destroy that.

Another positive result is that I am trying to become more
tolerant of individuals' differences of opinions and not simply
dismiss an idea as being crazy or ridiculous. Many people
have opened their hearts and minds in trying to accept the
reality of *my* experiences; I must learn to do the same for
others.

The alien abductions, mental flashes, and harassment by
military/government agents continue. I have learned to accept the alien abductions and am not frightened by them. My
biggest complaint against the aliens is they too often do not
allow me to recall the encounter consciously. I have, however, been given an explanation for this. One night as I was
verbally protesting the blockage of my memories, I was told,
"You are being monitored too closely by our opponents. Your
remembering would be detrimental to our mission."

Being told that a group of my abductors has opponents
led me to believe there is a great conflict going on in the
universe. Although I could be wrong, based on my continuing experiences, I now believe this conflict is between good
and evil in the struggle for our souls. I also have come to
believe that both good and evil are at every level: among
aliens, among humans, among our government and military.

Believing there are good people hidden somewhere within
our government and military agencies, I still harbor the hope
(or is it fantasy?) that someday one of these people will
approach me and voluntarily share information that will give

me a better understanding of the truth. For the truth is what I am after and will continue to seek.

NOTES

[1] Many names in this book have been changed to protect the privacy of the individuals involved. Pseudonyms are identified in parentheses or brackets at their first occurrence.

[2] For the protection of various people and organizations, the name of this town is fictitious, as well as the names of the university and military base located within it. However, all events described as taking place in this town are true. The names of all other locations mentioned in this book are real.

[3] Budd Hopkins, *Intruders: The Incredible Visitations at Copley Woods* (New York: Ballentine Books, 1989).

[4] Several UFO investigators have mentioned that perhaps Mike, Seth, and Mother were somehow prepared for my sudden involvement in the UFO phenomenon.

[5] *UFO Abduction Experiences—An Information Kit* (New York: Intruders Foundation, 1987).

[6] Budd Hopkins, "UFO Abductions—The Physical Dimension," *The Bulletin of the Intruders Foundation*, 1, No. 1 (Fall 1989), 6.

[7] Four assistants participated in my sessions at one time or another: Ann Bayliff, Susan Bedell, Lisa Dusenberry, and Carla Vincel. Because in transcribing the tapes of my sessions I found it sometimes impossible to distinguish the voice of one assistant from another, I used the name "Grace" to refer to all four in the text.

[8] I abbreviated quotes from hypnosis sessions, conversations, and letters in order to eliminate unnecessary repetition and immaterial matter. In some instances, I added or changed a few words and phrases to aid in the reader's understanding. However, in each case, I retained the substance of the thoughts, ideas, and spoken words so that the truth was preserved. All of my hypnosis sessions were taped; I transcribed the related tapes after returning home from each trip to Springfield.

About The Author

Leah A. Haley is also the author of *Ceto's New Friends* and a number of articles. She is a certified public accountant. She holds a bachelor's degree in secondary education from the University of Alabama, a master's degree in education from the University of North Alabama, and a master's degree in business administration from Mississippi State University. She practiced public accounting for several years before teaching a variety of university accounting courses. She now devotes all her time to writing and lecturing about the UFO/abduction phenomenon. She lives in Murfreesboro, Tennessee.

VISITORS FROM TIME

VISITORS FROM TIME
The Secret of the UFOs

New Revised Edition from Greenleaf Publications!

The Secret of the UFOs
Marc Davenport

Here is the most thoroughly documented book available in the UFO subject concerning the connection between UFOs and time travel! A must for every serious and not so serious scholar of ufology!

CONTACT FORUM
The round table of universal communication

Contact Forum was established as a vehicle for the open exchange of ideas and information, and it has succeeded in that mission!

Articles that have appeared in past issues are:

July/August 1993
- *Helping Abductees* by John E. Mack, M.D. author of *Abduction!*
- *No Intelligent Life is Alien to Me* by John R. Salter, Jr., Professor, University of North Dakota.

September/October 1993
- *Politically Correct Counseling of CE-IV Experiencers* by Richard J. Boylan, Ph.D, author of *Close Extraterrestrial Encounters.*
- *The Education of a Truth Seeker* by Donald Ware, a research Associate for CSETI.
- *Discovering Abductees and Other Startling Information* by Don Worley, UFO Investigator.

November/December 1993
- *Perceptions* by Brit Elders of Genesis III Publishers.
- *Stealing the Thunder* by Angela Thompson of the Bigelow Foundation.
- *A Tour of a UFO* by Michelle Lavigne, a lifelong experiencer.

January/February 1994
- Alien-inspired Art—several contributing artists.
- *An Appeal to the UFO Community* by Leah A. Haley, author of *Lost Was the Key.*

March/April 1994
- *Cosmic Wake-up Call* by Ann B. Livingston, Investigator and Spanish translator for MUFON.
- *Metamorphosis* by Edward Carlos, a Professor of fine arts, writer and also an experiencer.

May/June 1994
- Interview with David Jacobs, author of *Secret Life.*

Contact Forum publishes articles with different viewpoints.
Contact Forum believes the "truth" will be discovered by listening to all opinions.
Contact Forum also publishes articles anonymously…to protect people's privacy.
A subscription to **Contact Forum**
makes you a part of the process of solving the UFO mystery.

SO DON'T HESITATE…GET A SUBSCRIPTION TODAY AND JOIN IN THE DIALOG!

SUBSCRIPTION FORM—Yes! Please send **CONTACT FORUM** to:

Name_____

Address_____

City _____ State _____ Zip Code _____

Country _____ Telephone_____

MAIL TO:
Greenleaf Publications
P.O. Box 8152
Murfreesboro, TN 37133

check one of the following:

price per subscription:

- ☐ 1 year (6 issues) in the U.S. or its possessions $18.50
- ☐ 1 year in Canada $21.00
- ☐ 1 year outside the U.S. and Canada $24.75

- ☐ 2 years (12 issues) $33.00
- ☐ 2 years $40.00
- ☐ 2 years $46.50

TOTAL amount enclosed (in U.S. funds) is: _____

I am paying by ☐ check ☐ money order ☐ charge to: ☐ MasterCard ☐ Visa (No._____

Exp. Date _____) Signature _____

Write us for a FREE CATALOG of books and tapes about UFOs & alien contact